'Roderick Strange invites us to join him in the adventure of the liturgical year. He faces the challenges to belief with an engaging honesty and a wisdom enriched by his love of the gospel, his knowledge of the human heart and his gift of friendship.'

Timothy Radcliffe, OP

'The author shows a respectful attentiveness to the text of the Scriptures, and to the Catholic tradition; Strange faces, with immense honesty, all the difficulties and problems that people have with Catholic Christianity. This may be his best book yet.'

Nicholas King, SJ

'Roderick Strange brings together, in an elegant and engaging way, the experiences and treasures of a lifetime. With warmth and sensitivity, he offers to our contemporaries an exploration of Christian faith and hope which brings light to our troubled world. This is a delightful and rewarding book: an eloquent Catholic apologia.'

Cardinal Vincent Nichols

Journey into Light

*The Challenge and Enchantment
of Catholic Christianity*

RODERICK STRANGE

HODDER

First published in Great Britain in 2021 by Hodder & Stoughton
An Hachette UK company

This paperback edition first published in 2022

1

A CIP catalogue record for this title is available from the British Library

Paperback ISBN 978 1 529 38001 9
eBook ISBN 978 1 529 38002 6

Typeset in Bembo MT by Hewer Text UK Ltd, Edinburgh
Printed and bound in Great Britain by Clays Ltd, Elcograf S.p.A.

Hodder & Stoughton policy is to use papers that are natural, renewable and recyclable products
and made from wood grown in sustainable forests. The logging and manufacturing processes
are expected to conform to the environmental regulations of the country of origin.

Hodder & Stoughton Ltd
Carmelite House
50 Victoria Embankment
London EC4Y 0DZ

www.hodderfaith.com

For Paul Murray, OP

Contents

Preface

Before Brendan Walsh became the editor of the international Catholic Weekly, *The Tablet*, he was the publishing director of Darton, Longman and Todd. As director, he published three books of mine and he also oversaw the reissuing of a fourth, *The Catholic Faith*, that had been published originally by Oxford University Press in 1986. It had been well received, but a few years after the reissue Brendan suggested to me that it now needed to be revised with new examples and so forth. I could see what he meant and considered the suggestion carefully, but eventually I decided that the task was beyond me. The spoken word floats away on the breeze, but *litera scripta manent*, what has been written remains written.

At the same time, while considering the suggestion, I became aware of other material that I had accumulated over the past twenty years, homilies I had preached, talks I had given and, since 2002, contributions I have made virtually every month to the Credo column in *The Times* Register section on Saturdays. I have now written more than two hundred such pieces. My original remit for them was to be homiletic, to consider the Scripture readings that people might be hearing if they were going to church that weekend and to use them as a prompt for what I might write. And so the idea came to me, not to publish a collection of those *Times* pieces, which now would probably seem stale and out of date, but rather to mine them for ideas, stories and images that, with the other material, might offer a fresh presentation of Catholic Christianity. That might achieve what Brendan had had in mind; and I decided to use the Church's year from Advent to November as a frame of reference, which is what I have attempted here.

It may help, therefore, at the start to be aware of the shape of that year, the liturgical year. I see it as falling into three main sections. First, there is Advent and the Christmas season. Later, there is Lent and Eastertide. Finally, there is a third section which is known as Ordinary Time, but which is actually divided in two, the weeks between the end of the Christmas season and the start of Lent and then after Eastertide it resumes for about six months until Advent is due to begin once more, either at the end of November or early in December. The penitential and festive seasons, Advent and Christmas, Lent and Easter, supply obvious focal points, but Ordinary Time is rather more elusive. The earlier part I have used as an opportunity to pause and take stock; then for the later, lengthy period, I have chosen not to proceed through it, week by week, blow by blow, feast by feast, but instead to view it as a chance to consider Christian teaching and Christian living more generally, reflecting on what it means to become kingdom, to show mercy, and to reform and renew the Church. So this book, which is not at all a liturgical textbook, is conceived rather, as its title declares, as a journey into light.

This journey, of course, is not without its challenges. It implies a summons at the start to follow Jesus of Nazareth into the wilderness and then a readiness to serve those who are most in need in society, and to share as well in Jesus' sufferings, not least when the path he has marked out comes at times to be betrayed by selfishness and sin – our own and others who claim to be his followers. And yet facing those challenges also lends enchantment to the journey. To follow faithfully, in spite of our failures and our experiences of darkness and disaster, is to discover unlooked for, unimagined, blessings, portrayed unforgettably for me by Piero della Francesca's image of the Christ, stepping powerfully and confidently out of his tomb into the light.

Piero della Francesca, *The Resurrection*

★

Like all writers, I have many debts. Besides Brendan whose suggestion triggered the idea for this book, I am grateful to Ian Brunskill for inviting me to write those Credo articles for *The Times* in the first place and so causing me to gather together much of the material that I have now been able to revisit. And I am grateful as well to all my subsequent editors at *The Times*, up to the most recent, Damian Arnold, for supporting me and for giving me permission to make use of material from those articles here. Part of the fascination, naturally enough, of preparing the articles was being unsure who would be reading them. Would they be Christians or not? Believers or not? How could I make sense of what I was trying to say to whoever might read them? It was like firing arrows into the dark. Who knows where they might land? Awareness of the unknown readership has also guided what follows here. I have enjoyed the challenge which has been rewarded through letters from readers.

While preparing the book, two friends, John Breen and Charlie Clarke-Jervoise, read the draft, chapter by chapter, from their different perspectives, offering clear-sighted, perceptive advice and making suggestions that helped me to clarify what I was trying to say. And when the book had been finished, another friend, Timothy Radcliffe, read the whole text straight through with enthusiasm. I am grateful to them all and deeply appreciative of their help. Such support on a project like this is invaluable.

I thank, too, Caroline Michel, my friend of many years and now my agent, who has encouraged and advised me consistently and shrewdly, and Andy Lyon and Jessica Lacey and all the team at Hodder whose expertise has made the publication of this book possible.

Finally, I thank my Irish Dominican friend, Paul Murray, whose unfailing friendship over many years has been such a boon to me. It was Paul who suggested the title for this book. For that, but also for much kindness besides, I am now delighted to dedicate this book to him.

I

Believing in God

Tom Rickman was a valued friend of mine. He died in 2018. Tom was a gifted screenplay writer, nominated, for example, for an Academy Award for the script he wrote for *The Coal Miner's Daughter* that was released to great acclaim in 1980. Mild and modest, his range of interests and his knowledge were formidable. Among those interests was religion, although he would have considered himself to be agnostic and he once remarked to a friend of his and mine that he was surprised at my believing in God. He never mentioned his puzzlement to me, but I suppose that, like many people today, especially in western society, while fascinated by religion, he felt at a loss to understand how anyone who was reasonably well educated, could be committed to Christianity. Were he still alive, I'd be encouraging him to read Rupert Shortt's wise work, *God is No Thing*.[1] So, before starting out on this journey into light, it may be worth my while to say something about the way I think about God. I am not imagining myself to be offering some definitive proof of God's existence, but rather saying something about my understanding of the God in whom I believe. And I shall offer, as well, a thought on what is for so many people a major obstacle to their believing: the presence of evil in our world.

★

1 Rupert Shortt, *God is No Thing: Coherent Christianity*, (London, Hurst and Company, 2016).

Without, therefore, intending to supply an exhaustive account, like other Christians I believe that God, who is the creator of everything that exists, is personal, intelligent and loving, and that God has revealed himself to us. What sense can be made of such a statement?

Consider, first, the notion of God as personal. In 1980 the Dominican theologian, Herbert McCabe, was invited to give a short series of lectures at the university Catholic chaplaincy in Cambridge. His first lecture, 'God and Creation', was characteristically brilliant, profound and clear, reflecting on the way we should be thinking about God. He explained that, if God is the answer to the question how everything exists, then he cannot be included in that 'everything'. God is not one thing existing among others. 'It is not possible,' he stated pungently, 'that God and the universe should add up to make two.'[2] Then as a conclusion to this lecture, he turned to this question of God as personal: 'What are we to make of the notion of a "personal" God?' His reply was particularly striking.

McCabe makes two crucial points. He begins by acknowledging the way the idea of a 'personal' God can evoke an image of God as like a human person; an image, as he says, 'which may be useful but could evidently be misleading'. It can mislead, for instance, when our language of God as all-powerful or all-knowing reduces God to being a kind of superman. God is not Clark Kent. But then McCabe goes on to say – in a remark I found immediately illuminating – that people may call God personal 'because it seems absurd to say he is impersonal'. And he explains: 'However romantic we may get about the great impersonal forces of nature that seem to tower over us, we know perfectly well that they don't. What is impersonal and non-intelligent will, in principle, always obey us if only we know the trick.'[3] So, in the first

2 Herbert McCabe, *God Matters*, (London, Geoffrey Chapman, 1987), p.6.
3 McCabe, *God Matters*, p.8

2

place, when we speak of God as personal, we are not identifying God as a person, simply in the same way that human beings are persons. And secondly, when we speak of God as personal, we are letting go of concepts that confine God. We do not know what it means to call God personal, except to say that it enables us to escape from thinking of God as impersonal, which would have placed him ultimately under our control. God as personal is mystery, not in the sense of being a profound puzzle to be solved, but as a being we are invited to gaze upon and contemplate.

Believing in God as personal is, therefore, a delicate exercise. It helps us escape the absurdity of the impersonal, but it can also mislead. Nevertheless, as McCabe mentions, it can be useful as well, for Christians believe that God who is personal is the creator of all and intelligent and loving. To recognise God as the creator of all is, of course, not a scientific statement. Creating should be distinguished from making. When scientists eventually come to discover the physical process that explains how all that exists came to be made, they will not be discovering a creative divine finger on the button that set that process in motion. Creation is distinct from physics; it is of a different order. It is mystery and, when we speak of it, we are not presuming to define that mystery's mechanics. And the personal divine creator, the God who, we believe, is mystery and intelligent and loving, has created us, who are human, as beings who are gifted with intelligence and a capacity for loving. And, if that is the case, then something else seems to follow. There is a consequence, and the consequence is revelation.

★

Imagine a supreme being who is personal, intelligent and loving, who has created beings who are analogously persons and endowed with intelligence and a capacity for loving. Is it possible that, after creating such beings, the supreme being whom we call God, would not form a relationship with them, communicate with them? I suppose it is conceivable. Who knows what might be possible? But the overwhelming probability has to be that God, having created these personal beings who are capable of knowing and loving, having created them, as we say, in his own image and likeness, would indeed form with them a relationship of knowledge and love. In other words, he would communicate with them. He would reveal himself. And Christians, to state the obvious, believe that that revelation is made real supremely in Jesus of Nazareth who is the Christ. Supremely, but not exclusively. We are able to recognise a broader relationship as well, a relationship between the creator and creation. 'Life itself in the world then,' in a telling remark of another Dominican theologian, Edward Schillebeeckx, 'belongs to the very content of God's inner word to us. It interprets dimly at least something of that which God personally, by the attraction of grace, is whispering in our hearts.'[4] God is whispering in human hearts.

So religious experience is not something unique to Christians. While not every experience that is claimed as religious may be authentic, it is also true that many are. We need to recognise what that implies. If genuine religious experience is always ultimately by definition experience of God and if authentic religious experience is to be acknowledged among those who are not Christians, among Jews and Muslims and Buddhists and Hindus and others, indeed wherever authentic religious experience is recognised, then that experience, because it is authentic, can only be an experience of the one true God. There is no other God to authenticate it. As the Second Vatican Council declared: 'All nations are one community and have one origin, because God caused the whole human race to dwell on the

4 Edward Schillebeeckx, *Christ the Sacrament of the Encounter with God*, (A Sheed and Ward Book, Lanham, The Rowman and Littlefield Publishers, Inc, 1963), p.8.

whole face of the earth . . . The Catholic Church rejects nothing of those things which are true and holy in these religions.'[5]
We must do more than respect the good that can be discerned
in other faiths; indeed we must do more even than respect the
good to be found wherever people of goodwill, even without
any profession of religious faith whatsoever, act conscientiously
and well; for wherever we find such genuine goodness, we must
acknowledge as its origin the source of all that is good, the divine
presence, God whispering in human hearts.

★

To recognise God's presence elsewhere, however, should not
make us indifferent to the way we recognise his presence among
us, the revelation that we find according to Christian belief made
real supremely in Jesus of Nazareth. And the image of God
whispering in our hearts is engaging. It suggests not merely the
communication of information, but something more personal.
As that declaration on the Church's relationship with non-
Christian religions goes on to say, the Church is bound to preach
Christ unceasingly, since he 'is "the way, the truth and the life"
(John 14:6), in whom people find the fullness of religious life
and in whom God has reconciled all things to Himself'.[6]

The basis for that claim and what makes that revelation
supreme is our relationship with Jesus as our brother and our
conviction about the relationship in him of the divine and the
human. Christians believe that Jesus is a human being like any
one of us, while believing also that he is divine. He is not
called divine by a kind of poetic licence. He is truly God from
God, Light from Light, true God from true God. And in Jesus

5 *Nostra Aetate,* Declaration on the Church's Relation to non-Christian
Religions, nn.1, 2. Quotations from Council documents are taken from
Norman P. Tanner and Giuseppe Alberigo et al. (eds.) *Decrees of the
Ecumenical Councils,* English edition, (London, Sheed and Ward, 1990).
6 *Nostra Aetate,* n.2.

God became man. God the Father did not disguise himself in human form as Jesus; in Jesus the Word of God assumed human nature so as to reveal the Father's unfailing love for us. Jesus is as human as if he were not divine, as divine as if he were not human. Both natures, the human and the divine, retain their integrity, while they are united perfectly in him. Such a belief is breathtaking and can seem bewildering, but it offers us, in fact, a way of understanding the relationship between the secular and the sacred: the Bible is human writing, but also the Word of God; the Church is a human institution, but is also the people of God, the body of Christ; sacraments are symbolic human actions, but are divine as well, God's acts of love for us, effecting what they symbolise, such as new birth in Christ through baptism, and spiritual nourishment and a share in Christ's death and resurrection through the Eucharist; and indeed our vocation to holiness, to sharing in the divine nature, is a call to be fully human, not less human. In other words, each of these aspects of Catholic Christian faith reflects the pattern revealed in Jesus Christ, the Word of God made flesh.

*

If we can understand God as personal, as a mystery to be contemplated, if we can recognise that the making of what exists needs to be distinguished from its creation, and if we can make sense of God's presence and divine revelation as capable of being discerned in nature and in authentic religious traditions wherever they may be found, and, most of all, in the person of Jesus, truly divine and truly human, one difficulty still remains as a major obstacle, preventing many people from believing in God: the problem of evil. People ask, if believers can see the hand of God in every good thing that happens to them, however small, how can they claim that evil, for example, the disease eating away at the sight of some child in Africa, as Stephen Fry once remarked, is not also God's will? For some people, the presence of evil makes belief in God impossible. Evil appals us. However, it need not strike us dumb.

The real difficulty is not, of course, moral evil. Deceit and betrayal, terrorism and torture, war and violence, the hurt – whether physical or psychological, sexual or spiritual – which men and women inflict on one another; all of these are consequences of our freedom of choice. We have to take responsibility for those actions. The real problem arises from innocent suffering, the devastation caused by natural disasters, famine and drought, earthquake and flood, starvation and sickness, that disease eating away at a child's sight. How can a loving God permit such catastrophes?

It is a powerful question, rising up from a well of compassion. All the same, the question is flawed. At its root is a presumption about the nature of God and of God's power that is misconceived. God is said to be all powerful. And so, the argument goes, if this loving God is all powerful, why does he not exercise his power to prevent such tragedies? Wouldn't we, if we could? But we can't. Our power is limited. But God's, if he is all powerful, is not. If a loving God exists, why doesn't he act? Either God is not loving or not all powerful. But the flaw lies in supposing that God's power is just like ours, only greater.

I do not pretend to know much about divine power, but I am confident that there are two things I do know. The first is that I do not know what divine power is like; and the second is that, whatever it is like, it is not just an excess of human power. As I have mentioned already, God is not Clark Kent. When we call God all powerful, we do not mean that God is superman, possessing the extra muscle to do what we cannot. We may wonder why a different world was not created, one in which disasters never occur, a world entirely free from tragedy. But that is not our world. How would we have evolved in such a world? And as we become more aware of ecology and of the way we are integrated into this world, then we should realise that this is the world of which we have to make sense, the one

7

in which we actually live, the world in which we have been formed, not one conjured up by our visions of perfection.

In spite of its limitations, true of all analogies, there is one in these circumstances that I find helpful. Our world is not like a stage set upon which we are like actors on tour, playing these roles here in this place, but moving on and playing them again elsewhere next week in another theatre. To continue the analogy, we are more like film actors on location, a part of the natural environment. And we are a part of this world which is our natural setting. To survive elsewhere we would have to duplicate it. Think of the preparations necessary when people travel into space. We are not citizens of the Moon or Martians. This is our climate, these are the conditions that give us the life that we need for survival. We have come to exist because of this climate, these conditions. This is our world. Sometimes, it is true, our circumstances are terrible, famine and drought, earthquake and flood, starvation and sickness. A world without them would be wonderful. But, pace Shakespeare, all the world is not a stage. We are on location. This is our world. To return to Herbert McCabe, 'God cannot *interfere* in the universe, not because he has not the power but because, so to speak, he has too much; to interfere you have to be an alternative to, or alongside, what you are interfering with. If God is the cause of everything, there is nothing he is alongside. Obviously God makes no difference to the universe; we do not appeal specifically to God to explain why the universe is this way rather than that, for this we need only to appeal to explanations within the universe.'[7]

And if God is loving, where is he in all this? God is not some giant puppet master in the sky, manipulating or directing or ignoring events. He is in Jesus. God has not created us and turned away, callous and bored. He has not abandoned us. Jesus, the Father's Son, came to share our climate and our

7 McCabe, *God Matters*, p.6.

conditions. He knew hunger and thirst, exhaustion and sorrow. He was put to death indeed because of human malice, moral evil, but he was, par excellence, the innocent victim. For some, evil blinds them to God's presence. For others, as we shall explore in Passiontide, Jesus makes it plain that there is no evil – physical, moral, or spiritual – that is beyond redemption.

*

For me, therefore, God is mystery and God is loving. God has created all that exists and has created everything out of love. I would not attempt to define God. I gaze and I contemplate. Some years ago, while praying one morning I was suddenly arrested, as I had never been before, by the account of Moses seeing the bush burning at Mount Horeb, the bush that was afire, but not consumed (Exodus 3:2). I am not implying that I had any kind of mystical experience, but what an image for God, the bush afire but unconsumed. The power of the image stayed with me and nourished my praying for some weeks, and I can return to it again and again to be refreshed.

And God, cloaked in mystery, is all knowing. What I have said about divine power, I would echo about divine knowledge. I know two things about it: first, that I do not know what divine knowledge is; second, I know it is not simply superhuman knowledge, God possessing answers to all the questions we cannot fathom. Divine knowledge is of a kind utterly beyond that. And this God of knowledge and love has revealed himself indeed, in many ways, but supremely in the birth and life, death and resurrection of Jesus of Nazareth who is truly divine, the Son of God, but also truly human, truly one of us. As we have affirmed already and as we shall explore further later, he has shared our condition and revealed God's unlimited love for us, and, by doing so, opened up for us our journey into light.

2

Advent: preparing the way

'Stay awake': the cry rings out like a clarion call at the start
of Advent. But, when we check the reference, we discover
that these words are not spoken at the start of the Gospel
narrative, but by Jesus towards the end of his ministry, when
he warns his followers to be on the alert for the last days and
for judgment (see Matthew 24:42; Mark 13:33; Luke 21:36).
So why should we be asked to listen to them now? Isn't
Advent a beginning, the time when we prepare to celebrate
the start of this new life, the Saviour's birth at Christmas?
Indeed it is. Nevertheless these are also appropriate words as
the Advent season begins, for, although they refer immediately to the end time, they can also stir us to look back to
that momentous birth two thousand years ago. We should be
alert, ready to learn what it can teach us. And there is more,
because we look back most effectively by examining ourselves
here and now. To put it simply, Advent invites us to engage
with a triple perspective: we must stay awake for the judgment that is to come, stay awake to explore the present
moment, alert to Christ's presence in our midst now, at this
time, and, in so doing, stay awake to celebrate Jesus' birth
long ago. Advent is a rich season. We need to be alert, watching and waiting. And two people dominate it: Mary, the
mother of Jesus, and John the Baptist. Let us consider the
Baptist first.

*

John is known as the forerunner of Jesus, the herald who went before him. Even the account of his birth foreshadows that of Jesus.

According to the Gospel of Luke, John's parents were Zechariah and Elizabeth. They had had no children and both were elderly. Zechariah was a priest. One day, when he was fulfilling his priestly duty in the sanctuary, he had a vision. An angel is said to have appeared to him and told him, 'Your wife Elizabeth will bear you a son, and you will name him John. You will have joy and gladness, and many will rejoice at his birth, for he will be great in the sight of the Lord.' Zechariah was overwhelmed with fear. He replied, 'How will I know that this is so? For I am an old man, and my wife is getting on in years.' The angel then identified himself as Gabriel, an archangel of God, and informed him: 'Because you did not believe my words, which will be fulfilled in their time, you will become mute, unable to speak, until the day these things occur' (Luke 1:5–20).

Zechariah's silence has often been understood as a punishment for his reluctance to believe the angel, but I would suggest that this notion is misconceived. As we shall see, the mother of Jesus in similar circumstances asks a similar question, but is neither rebuked nor punished. It makes better sense to recognise Zechariah's silence as part of a sign of what is to come. His son, John, as the herald of the Christ, is to be known as the 'voice' that cries out in the wilderness, preparing the way for the Lord. What does a voice effect? St Augustine offered a moving explanation centuries later: 'John was a voice, but the Lord in the beginning was the Word ... The sound of the voice brings you to understand the word. And when the voice has done this, it ceases; but the word carried to you by the sound is now already in your heart, and has not left mine.'[1] At

---

1 Augustine, Sermon 293, 3, *The Divine Office* i, (London, Collins, 1974), p.98.

the birth of John, the voice, his father recovers his own voice. His silence has been a sign.

When John then appears in the Judean wilderness, his dress and his diet are described. He is wearing a garment of camel's hair and eating locusts and wild honey. What a strange figure he must have made, yet people flocked to him and bombarded him with questions. They wanted to know who he was. Was he the Messiah? Or Elijah? Or a prophet? Each question he dismissed out of hand. He had come, rather, he told them, quoting the prophet Isaiah, to prepare the way of the Lord. He was, he declared (now we hear it), 'the voice of one crying in the wilderness, "Make straight the way of the Lord"' (John 1:19–23). And he was to make that way straight not least by calling people to repentance. What does that repentance involve?

Isaiah's words appear in all the Gospels, but only Luke continues them. There we read, 'Every valley shall be filled and every mountain and hill shall be brought low, and the crooked shall be made straight, and the rough ways shall be made smooth; and all flesh shall see the salvation of God' (Luke 3:5–6; Isaiah 40:3–4). Filling valleys and flattening hills is an arresting image. What are we to make of it? Perhaps we should understand these words not as referring to some physical landscape, an improbable engineering project, but to a landscape within. As we examine ourselves, where are the hills and valleys in our hearts, the rough roads and the winding ways? Are we hiding in the hills or skulking in the valleys? Are we content to travel on rough roads, because the vibrations blur our vision, and to follow winding ways because twists and turns help us to avoid our responsibilities? So the image can be seen as something personal, a call to personal repentance, personal conversion. We have to prepare the way of the Lord in our own hearts and that can be demanding.

Those demands were explained entertainingly some years ago by a friend of mine, Peter Steele, an Australian Jesuit who died in 2012. Peter was driving in Ireland in 1977 and stopped for a pub lunch. Soon after, a man who had been working on the road outside the pub, came in and insisted on buying Peter a drink. Peter felt he could afford the hospitality far more easily than his new companion, but the man was having none of it. A typical Irishman, he was a model of generosity. But the experience also prompted Peter in a homily he preached years later to illustrate Christian repentance. 'When you are mending roads,' he observed, 'you rip them up a good deal before you smooth them out: the smoothing won't be much good without the ripping.' And that, he continued, was what John was doing.[2] He was ripping open the hearts of those listening to him, preparing them to become better people.

The people, whom John was upbraiding, excoriating as a brood of vipers, far from taking offence, ask him further questions. They want to know what they must do. And he tells them: they should share what they possess with those who are in need. He instructs the tax collectors, who were renowned for charging excessive amounts so that the percentage they could claim might increase, that they should 'collect no more than the amount prescribed' for them; and he warns the soldiers not to extort money from anyone by threats or false accusations, and to be satisfied with their wages (see Luke 3:10–14). So they are to look not only into their own hearts, but also they are to examine how they treat others.

We shall be meeting John again, but for the moment, as we prepare to set out on our journey into light, we can try to take those lessons to heart. We repent by trying to know ourselves better, by exploring the hills and valleys in which we may hide, and, even if we aren't tax collectors or corrupt soldiers, whatever our responsibilities in life may be, by trying to serve better those who are in need.

*

2 Peter Steele, *Bread for the Journey*, (Melbourne, David Lovell Publishing, 2002), p.7.

The second person to dominate the Advent season is Mary, the mother of Jesus. It could be said we meet her even before she was born, because on 8 December the feast of her immaculate conception is celebrated. But what that means has often caused confusion.

Many people imagine the conception referred to is the conception of Jesus, dubbed 'immaculate' because Mary was a virgin. It seems, therefore, to underscore what is sometimes perceived as Christian negativity about sex. But that is a mistake. This conception is Mary's, a conception that was unexceptional, taking place in the normal sexual manner. It is called immaculate because she is believed to have been born without the stain of original sin which, as we shall reflect later, is not another category of sin, but a way of speaking about the origin of human sinning. And if that all seems rather obscure, it is worth noting that most people in modern secular society believe in the immaculate conception, as they have no time for the notion of original sin. If you don't believe in original sin, then every conception is immaculate.

Part of the problem with this teaching as it is often presented, however, may be caused by language which is static and negative. How much more powerful the teaching becomes when presented positively and dynamically as the celebration of a life that is overwhelmed by faith in God and love for God. That is the Mary we meet in Advent.

The scene is familiar. In Luke's Gospel the angel Gabriel appears to the young girl and addresses her: 'Greetings, favoured one. The Lord is with you.' We are familiar, too, with the great paintings that have depicted the scene. It has inspired some of the world's finest artists, Fra Angelico, Titian, Caravaggio and others. A favourite of mine that fires my imagination is one that is more recent. It is by Henry Ossawa Tanner, an African-American painter, who was born in 1859 and died in 1937. For many years he worked in Paris. In 1898 he produced his startling impression of the Annunciation.

Henry Ossawa Tanner, *The Annunciation*

For me this painting captures something of Mary's awe and bewilderment and sense of mystery. The girl looks rather dazed. Has she just been roused from sleep? Her clothes and bed are bathed in golden light. There is a warm, red backcloth. Her pale, oval face is lowered, though her gaze, bemused but also calm, is raised to the shimmering angelic light that hovers near her.

Luke's account, of course, is not supplying us with a bald description of an event, a kind of verbal photograph. That is rarely the Bible's priority. It is trying rather to convey the significance of the experience. Mary is praised as favoured, full of grace. The exchange between her and the angel that follows reveals the unique nature of what she is being invited to do. Though a virgin, she is being asked to bear a child who is to be the 'Son of the Most High'. Because she is a virgin, just as Zechariah had done because he was old, she questions what she is being told. 'How can this be?' she exclaims. The angel reassures her: 'The Holy Spirit will come upon you, and the power of the Most High will overshadow you; therefore the child to be born will be holy; and he will be called Son of God.' There is no hint that her question was prompted by a lack of faith, a refusal to accept the angel's message. Nor was it. And she is given a sign. And for her the sign, like Zechariah's silence, is that her relative, Elizabeth, the wife of Zechariah, although old, has conceived and will bear a son. And Mary replies, 'Behold, I am the handmaid of the Lord; let it be to me according to your word' (Luke 1:38 RSV).

The teaching that Mary, the mother of Jesus, though a virgin, conceived her son without losing her virginity may seem laughably implausible today. Nevertheless, it has been affirmed in the Church since the earliest times, not to safe-guard the Christ's divinity, nor because of a failure to affirm his true humanity, nor either because of a defective view of human sexuality, but because it was accepted as true.[3] Besides the texts in the New Testament, there is evidence from the beginning of the second century. St Ignatius of Antioch, for example, refers to Jesus being 'truly born of a virgin', in the same way that he refers to Jesus' baptism by John and his crucifixion.[4] But, for the sake of argument, let us suppose that this is a mistake. Let us suppose, which is not possible, that we could be privy to the most intimate aspects of Mary's relationship with Joseph, her husband, and discovered that Jesus' conception took place in the normal, sexual way. What difference would that make? Nothing. Why? Because the teaching about the virginal

3 For a fuller exploration of how this doctrine is understood, see my previous book: Roderick Strange, *The Catholic Faith*, (London: DLT, 2001), pp.168–70.
4 Ignatius of Antioch, 'Letter to the Smyrnaeans', 1, Maxwell Staniforth (translator), *Early Christian Writings: The Apostolic Fathers*, (Penguin Books, Ltd., 1982,) p.119.

conception of Jesus is not primarily about Mary's physical condition, but is rather a way of speaking about God's action, that this child was sent by God (Galatians 4:4). Believing in the virginal conception of Jesus is a way of affirming the divine initiative.

And once the vision was over, we are told that Mary set out to visit Elizabeth. On her arrival she was greeted with words with which so many of us have become familiar: 'Blessed are you among women, and blessed is the fruit of your womb.' But, we are told, Elizabeth also declared to her, 'Blessed is she who believed that there would be a fulfilment of what was spoken to her by the Lord' (Luke 1:42, 44). Those are words that touch the heart. And so, as we move through this Advent season, preparing ourselves, it is good to try to hear those words addressed to Mary as words addressed also to everyone who believes: 'Blessed are those who believe that the promise made to them by the Lord would be fulfilled.' We hear those words and can be buoyed up by the promise they proclaim.

*

In 1100 or thereabouts, Isaac of Stella was born in England. He became a monk in France, in due course a Cistercian, influenced by Bernard of Clairvaux. His name, Stella, de l'Etoile, is taken from a small village, Stella, north-east of Poitiers, where he became abbot of the local monastery. In a well-known sermon he spoke about how both Mary and the Church are the mother of Christ. He declared: 'Mary gave birth to the absolutely sinless Head for the Body; the Church gave birth, in the forgiveness of every sin, to the Body for the Head. Each is the mother of Christ, but neither without the other gives birth to the whole Christ.'[5] Mary and the Church are united in giving birth to the Christ. And the promise given to us is to be

5 Isaac of Stella, 'Sermon 51', *The Divine Office*, i, p.95.

the body of Christ. How, then, are we to live, if we believe that the promise made to us by the Lord would be fulfilled?

In the circumstances it might be tempting to offer a clear, cut-and-dried answer, a set of rules to be followed so that all would be well, but that would miss the point. How often those who think they have all the answers have failed to grasp properly the question. We must move beyond a mindset that deals only with what can be defined clearly and have the courage to face up to ambiguity. That is the path Pope Francis is indicating. Faithful to the tradition of the Church, he is conscious at the same time of the complex reality of the human condition. To be the Church that we are called to be means having the courage to live in accordance with that reality. And there is something else to notice here.

People, as we know, often remark on the contrast between religion and science, the one seen as vague and obscure, while the other deals in clarity and reliable evidence. How refreshing it was, therefore, on Sunday 26 April, in the midst of the coronavirus pandemic in 2020, to hear Professor Brian Cox being interviewed on *The Andrew Marr Show* on the BBC. Cox, a physicist and a television presenter, was having to homeschool his own children at the time and was acknowledging how difficult that could be. But he also commented on life in the pandemic. He noted that those who refer to 'the science' – citing the common mantra that 'We have to follow "the science"' – don't in fact understand what science is about. It does not supply a set of smart answers, but, he said, it refers to a mindset, a way of understanding nature. And at the heart of that understanding is the recognition that doubt and uncertainty are to be embraced and welcomed, not feared. We have to face the unknown and explore it.

What doubts and uncertainty the mother of Jesus had to face. The angel's message must have bewildered her. The initial doubt of Joseph, her betrothed, who planned to divorce her, must have caused her distress. And no doubt there was local gossip as well. And then, according to Luke, there was the long journey from Nazareth to Bethlehem and there was much else she would have to endure in the future. Yet she never faltered. She believed that the promise made to her by the Lord would be fulfilled. She gave us an example that we can follow.

★

Guided then by John the Baptist and the mother of Jesus, we begin our journey into light by making our way through the Advent season. We hear John's call to repentance and may well be in awe of Mary's faith. Penitence and awe are challenging. Can we measure up to their demands? But they are not the only qualities that mark Advent. There is another and it may take us by surprise: it is joy, not trivial cheeriness, but something profound. To know that God so loved the world that he gave his only Son is an overwhelming truth. How could it not fill us with joy? How could we not respond to it? As St John Henry Newman once remarked in an Advent sermon: 'Let us never lose sight of two truths – that we ought to have our hearts penetrated with the love of Christ and full of self-renunciation.'[6]

Self-renunciation does not mean self-hatred or low self-esteem. It refers rather to a readiness to know ourselves as we truly are, a readiness to embrace genuine self-knowledge. We know we are not perfect, but we can be at ease with ourselves, not conceited or arrogant. It is the repentance to which the Baptist calls us. And blessed with that self-knowledge and with hearts filled with love for Christ we rejoice. We rejoice because we recognise that we are loved by God. We rejoice because, being loved, we seek to respond to God's will as faithfully as Mary. Joy is wonderful, but at the same time we need to brace ourselves. It is not only not trivial cheeriness; it will often go

6 J. H. Newman, 'Unreal Words', in *Parochial and Plain Sermons* v, uniform edition. (Westminster, Md, Christian Classics, Inc 1967), p.39.

hand-in-hand with hardship. In the words of Sister Mary David Totah, 'It is noteworthy how often in the New Testament joy and affliction go together.'[7] Let me tell you something about Sister Mary David.

★

I knew her first as Michele. She was an American, small, dark-haired, and full of fun and laughter. She was a graduate student at Oxford in the early 1980s, while I was chaplain. After completing her research, she had returned to the United States and was teaching as an associate professor at the College of Mary and William in Williamsburg, Virginia. Then one summer's afternoon in 1984 she called in to see me unannounced. She was wondering whether she might have a vocation to the religious life and, to help her reflect, she had taken the opportunity to visit a Benedictine monastery, St Cecilia's Abbey, on the Isle of Wight, before coming on to see friends in Oxford. She had chosen to go to St Cecilia's simply because she had never been before. But it was love at first sight. She was captivated and had come to talk to me about entering that community. She went back to the States to teach for a further year, but then returned and went to St Cecilia's in May 1985 – but not before causing some consternation at immigration. Asked how long she planned to stay in Britain, she replied with all the enthusiasm of a lover, 'For ever, I hope.' And she was promptly marched off to be interrogated as a suspected illegal immigrant.

In the monastery she was given the name Mary David and in 1996 she became its inspiring novice mistress, a role that she retained for the rest of her life. In 2008 she also became prioress. She was passionate, but gentle as well. Four years later she was diagnosed with cancer. When told, she declared, 'I gave

7 Mary David Totah, *The Joy of God*, (London, Bloomsbury Continuum, 2019), p.2.

God everything at my Profession. I give him this too.' She was ready for anything. Expected to live no more than two years, she survived for five, continuing to teach, continuing to be an inspiring presence in the monastery.

There is much more that could be said about Mary David and we will meet her again, but I offer this brief sketch because it is important to realise that her recognition of the way joy and affliction can go together is not to be understood as autobiography. She is not just talking about her cancer. She is thinking about the way trials and challenges are a part of all our lives and she is referring to the way Christian joy can flourish in the least favourable soil. There can be encouragement for us even in the midst of hardship. 'This joy in the midst of suffering,' she has written, 'is nothing other than the joy of love. It is not a question of loving suffering for itself, but of seeing the acceptance and overcoming of it, and even the choice of it, as a proof of love . . . We often think of the Cross as an obstacle to joy, as something barring the way to happiness. The saints are far simpler: for them joy means loving someone. This means they can suffer anything and still be happy.' And she adds, 'This kind of joy does involve renunciation; we have to lose ourselves in order to find ourselves and joy.'[8] So we are brought round to thinking of the Baptist's call to repentance, renunciation, and self-knowledge, as a call to joy.

Shortly afterwards, Mary David explained that joy is not something emotional, something simply that we feel, but something that we choose. In other words, it is rooted in desire, another truth to which we shall have to return. As she expressed it, 'joy is not something determined by our state of mind or situation; it lies far deeper than happiness or unhappiness, consolation or desolation, pleasure or pain. It is not something we feel, but something we do. It is something to be chosen, a

8 Totah, *The Joy of God*, pp. 3–4.

choice God calls us to. In calling us to himself, he calls us to joy, for he *is* our joy.'[9]

★

God is our joy. We are called to rejoice. And when Mary had received and accepted the angel's message, we are told that she went to visit Elizabeth, and on hearing Elizabeth's greeting, 'Why has this happened to me, that the mother of my Lord comes to me?' Mary replied, 'My soul magnifies the Lord and my spirit *rejoices* in God my Saviour' (Luke 1:46). And when her son was born, shepherds in the fields nearby had a vision of an angel who proclaimed to them, 'Do not be afraid; for see – I am bringing you good news of great *joy* for all the people: to you is born this day in the city of David a Saviour who is the Messiah, the Lord' (Luke 2:10–11).

Therefore, we prepare ourselves for our journey into light during Advent, a season that is marked by the call to renunciation, faith, and joy. Those qualities shape our disposition. And so we move into the Christmas season where we celebrate and explore the significance of Jesus' birth.

9 Totah, *The Joy of God*, p.9.

3

Christmas: a child is born

Sometimes, when I've been working with study groups or catechists, I've invited them to relate the sequence of events surrounding Christ's birth. The answer tends to go like this:

It begins with the angel Gabriel appearing to Mary in Nazareth and inviting her to become the mother of the child; after that she goes to visit her relative, Elizabeth. Joseph, her betrothed, then has a dream that puts his mind at rest about Mary's pregnancy and her faithfulness. Later, because of the census, they travel from Nazareth to Bethlehem but can find no room in any inn and the baby is born in a stable. Soon after the birth they are visited by shepherds who have been tending their flocks, and who tell them they have seen a vision of angels, who announced the child's birth. Then, eight days later they take the child to be circumcised in the temple in Jerusalem where they meet Simeon and Anna. Next, they are visited by the magi, wise men from the east, who bring them gifts of gold, frankincense and myrrh. After these visitors have left, however, Joseph learns in a dream that King Herod who has heard of the birth, plans to kill the child. So Joseph takes Mary and Jesus to safety in Egypt and, when he learns in another dream that Herod has died, he returns with them to Nazareth. That, in brief, is the account people tend to give of the Christmas story which is familiar to so many.

Then I ask the group, 'In which Gospel do these events occur?' A look of alarm can often cross their faces. Nativity narratives, as we know, occur only in the Gospels of Matthew and Luke, but the birth is the only feature common to them both. I reassure them, 'Don't worry. The baby is born in both the Gospels.' It is true that the family ends up in Nazareth, but while in Luke they are returning home after their meeting with Simeon and Anna, in Matthew they are going there for the first time on their return from Egypt. According to Matthew, their home originally is in Bethlehem. Matthew speaks of dreams, Luke of visions. The magi appear only in Matthew's Gospel, the shepherds and Simeon and Anna only in Luke's. Only in Matthew is there a flight into Egypt. The two Gospels have different priorities. Matthew's account is punctuated with quotations from the Old Testament: its concern is with fulfilment; Luke, on the other hand, entertains a larger vision, a message for everyone, captured by Simeon speaking of the child as 'a light for revelation to the Gentiles' (Luke 2:32).

The distinctive emphases in the two nativity narratives anticipate the principal themes in the Gospels as a whole: in Matthew, it is about fulfilment, in Luke it is the universal vision. It is instructive to be aware of these emphases. These narratives are not like newspaper reports. Their purpose is different. Each in its own way sets the scene so that the significance of this child can be understood.

*

In October 2019, I was fortunate enough to attend the canonisation of Cardinal John Henry Newman in Rome. On my return, those less fortunate than me, who had not been present, asked me what moment during that weekend of celebrations had been most memorable. Many might have expected me to speak about the canonisation ceremony itself, the solemnity of the Mass in St Peter's Square. But that occasion, splendid as it was, was not for me what stands out most of all. The evening before, there had been a liturgy in the Basilica of Santa Maria Maggiore.

As that liturgy began, all the lights were blazing in the Basilica so that the gold leaf on the walls was radiant and, as a long procession made its way down the aisle, the packed congregation burst into song, singing verses that Newman had composed in his poem, *The Dream of Gerontius*. They were singing, 'Praise to the Holiest in the Height.'[1] Tears came to my eyes. I was moved to see Newman so honoured in Rome where he had in his lifetime so often been misunderstood. But some words of the hymn, with which, of course, I was very familiar, suddenly struck me afresh. I felt as though I was hearing them for the first time, appreciating them more deeply than ever. They refer to the coming of the Saviour.

> O loving wisdom of our God,
> When all was sin and shame,
> A second Adam to the fight
> And to the rescue came.

Into a world scarred by sin and shame, wars and violence, terrorism and human trafficking, conflicts personal and domestic, greed and selfishness, into this world, a second Adam had come, not like the first who had injected into us an instinct for wrongdoing, an instinct that introduced us to sin and shame, but a second who had come to rescue and restore us. And how was that to be achieved? First, because human flesh and blood that had failed in the first Adam, should now 'strive afresh against the foe / Should strive and should prevail'. And again, we ask how? How can humanity

---

1 Cardinal Stanisław Ryłko, the Archpriest of the Basilica, is reported as saying he had never before heard singing in the Basilica like it.

now strive and prevail? And so, secondly, we are told of a higher gift than grace that we have received, one that refines human flesh and blood. There have been those who have questioned whether there is such a gift, one that is higher than grace. But there is:

> God's Presence and His very Self,
> And Essence all-divine.[2]

At Christmas, we celebrate the birth of this Jesus, the second Adam, the Christ-child. A human baby is born and as such is no different from any other. At the same time, Christians believe that this small child is also divine, refined by that gift higher than grace, though not in a way that compromises his humanity. He is no less human for being divine. He is not a divine being, like a god in mythology, who has come to visit humanity, but simply by adopting a human disguise. Nor is belief in his divinity a turn of speech, just a way of attributing exceptional, unique status to his humanity. When we speak of Jesus as divine, we are not indulging in poetic licence. His humanity is ordinary humanity. He is one of us. But he is also truly divine. Jesus is God. Yet we believe as well that these two natures, the human and the divine, are related in him in their integrity. The child is truly and fully human, truly and fully divine, without these natures in him being either confused or divided.[3] In spite of many difficulties and throughout many controversies that sought to tame the mystery that was being proclaimed, the Church has maintained this position consistently, namely that what it believed about the Christ could only be expressed satisfactorily by affirming his true humanity and his true divinity, while respecting the unity of those natures in

2 J. H. Newman, *Verses on Various Occasions*, uniform edition (London, Longmans, Green. and Co., 1896), pp.363–4.
3 See Strange, *The Catholic Faith*, pp.7–9.

him in their integrity. Nothing less would do. It is a wondrous belief. I remember a wise friend once saying to me that if, after all, this proved to be untrue, nevertheless, what an overwhelming idea it was. It lifted the heart. Who could have dreamt of such a concept? Who could not be in awe of it?

★

On Christmas Day the Eucharist is celebrated on three occasions, at midnight, at dawn, and then during the day, but these three Masses are not mere repetitions of each other.

At midnight we hear about the census decreed by Caesar Augustus, so that Joseph has to leave Nazareth with Mary, his betrothed, and go to Bethlehem to be registered there, since, we are told, he was of David's house and family. In the Lukan account, there is no room where they can stay in an inn and Mary gives birth to her child in a stable. How stressful and exhausting that time must have been for her. And then we hear of shepherds, watching their flocks in fields nearby who have a vision of an angel proclaiming the birth of the child, news of great joy 'to be shared by all the people'. They are terrified, but reassured by the angel. There the Gospel passage at midnight ends (Luke 2:1–14). A child has been born and the birth proclaimed.

At dawn, however, the narrative continues. The shepherds hurry to find the child and tell Mary and Joseph of their experience. They also spread the news to the local people in the town who are amazed by what they hear. But the crucial words at dawn speak of Mary's reaction. On hearing what the shepherds tell her, she 'treasured all these words and pondered them in her heart' (Luke 2:15–20).

Caravaggio, in his depiction of the shepherds coming to adore the child, captured tellingly Mary's exhaustion and wonder. At dawn we are invited to contemplate with Mary, pondering on what had taken place.

★

Caravaggio, *The Adoration of the Shepherds*

How are we to identify the newborn child? The accounts recorded according to Matthew, Mark, Luke, and John each have their own emphases and characteristics; the nativity narratives have offered us examples of diversity already. Yet there is something to be learned from a larger view.

Scholars nowadays would say that the earliest continuous sections of the Gospels to be written were the accounts of the Lord's Passion and resurrection. And then, naturally, the question arose: who was this Jesus who had been tortured and crucified and who had then been raised from the dead? An obvious way to answer it was to give an account of his life, in particular his ministry in the years leading to his death. Wouldn't that make plain who he was? And so narratives were written about certain events, what he had done and what he had said, his teaching and his parables, and the signs he gave, the miracles he had worked. Mark's Gospel, the earliest, supplied just such a narrative. And yet the answer that narrative supplied was not entirely satisfactory. An answer to the fundamental question had still to be found: who was Jesus? And so Matthew and Luke, as well as giving their versions of Jesus' mission and ministry, as Mark had done, added, as we have noticed already, nativity narratives with emphases which vary: Matthew focusing on fulfilment, Luke on a universal vision. Even that, however, proved not to be completely satisfying. Layers are being peeled away: from the death and resurrection of Jesus, to his ministry, and to his birth.

Nowadays, there are pilgrimages to Israel that begin in Nazareth and move south from Galilee to Jerusalem. They are following the course of the Lord's life chronologically, from childhood, through ministry, to death and resurrection. On a number of occasions, however, when I have been invited to accompany a group as its chaplain, we have taken the opposite route. We have begun in Jerusalem, taking time to reflect on Jesus' death and resurrection, before moving north into the Galilee, to meditate on his ministry and teaching in Capernaum and on the mount beside the sea of Galilee associated with the sermon that was delivered there, and his childhood in Nazareth. Neither route is perfect, but I have always been grateful that the route I was asked to follow made it possible to explore events more theologically, to explore Jesus' identity, from his Passion, death and resurrection through his ministry to his childhood in Nazareth. We were peeling back the layers. When we ponder on Jesus' birth, however, we have still not finished our exploring. There is more to be done.

*

At the third Mass, during the day, the perspective shifts again. We move from Luke's narrative, which is the one we have been hearing at midnight and dawn, and listen instead to the prologue of the fourth Gospel: 'In the beginning was the Word, and the Word was with God, and the Word was God . . . and the Word became flesh and lived among us' (John 1:1–14). Here there is a further development. We are peeling back yet another layer: the birth that was proclaimed at midnight and contemplated at dawn, as Mary treasured what the shepherds had told her and pondered it in her heart, now in the prologue it is unveiled as the mystery of the incarnation: Jesus is the Word of God, become flesh, and living among us.

And so we find that, to discover who Jesus is, Christians have moved indeed from reflecting at first on his Passion and resurrection to considering his public ministry and then on to exploring the accounts of the events surrounding his birth until they have arrived at this profound theological statement that introduces the last of the Gospels to be written: Jesus is the Word of God made flesh. We will never exhaust the wonder of this mystery; we must contemplate; there will always be more that can be uncovered. It took virtually another four hundred years before the Church articulated what it believed about Jesus in a definitive statement. That was at the Council of Chalcedon in 451.

Besides this declaration, however, that the Word who was God became flesh and lived among us, there is another theme in the prologue: that of witness. John the Baptist is mentioned. It is made plain that he himself is not the Word, the light that overcomes the world's darkness. Rather, he is the one who testifies to the light. In other words, John is the one who bears witness on behalf of the Word. At the Day Mass, therefore, as well as being led to a deeper appreciation of the identity of Jesus, the Word made flesh, we are confronted by this call to witness.

And the theme of witness now takes centre stage. The fundamental significance of Christmas is such that it is celebrated not only on that one day, but also for the seven days following. This eight-day period, the Christmas Octave, is to be seen as a single feast and at its heart, besides the birth, there is also the call to witness. Witnessing can take many forms.

*

St Stephen

The day after Christmas Day is popularly known as Boxing Day because in times past it was the day when servants received their Christmas boxes and were given the day off. Think of *Downton Abbey*. For Christians, however, 26 December is the feast of St Stephen, the first martyr. The word, martyr, taken from the Greek, means witness. And Stephen, a deacon in the early Church, is the first Christian recorded as having been executed for his faith (Acts 6:8–7:60). He was stoned to death. Within twenty-four hours we have moved from the birth of

Jesus to the death of Stephen, from womb to tomb. In a virtual echo of words that would be attributed to Jesus on the cross, 'Father, forgive them; for they do not know what they are doing' (Luke 23:34), Stephen exclaimed, 'Lord, do not hold this sin against them' (Acts 7:60). Stephen's death alerts us immediately to Jesus' destiny. He bore witness by giving up his life.

The Holy Family

When a Sunday occurs between Christmas Day and the New Year, it is celebrated as the feast of the Holy Family. It seems natural in these days to celebrate this family, Jesus, Mary and Joseph, not least because families often gather at Christmas and it is an opportunity for us to appreciate what our families give us. They are the original source of our social life. But at the same time we need to be wary of facile sentimentality. Our homes are filled with memories: many are joyful, but not all.

The old saying declares that charity begins at home. That may be true, but not because the family setting is one where life is always easy and conflict unknown. On the contrary, it may be much easier to star as charming and considerate on a visit to friends, while the family is a much tougher place to love. Our families know us well. Put on an act and they will see through it at once. All the same, while those who love us won't tolerate our nonsense, they will commonly be loyal. One fundamental lesson about loving that we learn from home teaches us the need for unselfish, faithful commitment.

If there is a desire common to the human heart it is to love and know that we are loved in return. That is a gift beyond compare. Secure and stable relationships are never to be undervalued. Perhaps some of the contemporary cynicism with regard to what is seen as conventional family life comes from our failure to recognise the cost at which it was won. Those of us, for example, born in the aftermath of the Second World War, were probably born to parents who were born during the First World War and who then fought in the Second. They were only too aware of society being at risk. When they married and had families, many of them worked hard to supply us, their children, with the security they themselves had not been able to enjoy. I sometimes wonder whether they did not achieve their aim so successfully that those of us born at that time have taken that security for granted, not realising the effort that was required to reach it. Taking it for granted, we may then have failed to create for our own children that stable setting that is vital if happiness is to flourish.

All this, of course, is at the individual, personal level. But even in the happiest of families there can be crises, sickness, bereavement and unemployment. In the Covid-19 pandemic, as we have seen, those elements presented an alarmingly united front. The virus has made many unwell, tragic numbers have died, and the series of lockdowns that have been put in place to combat the virus has damaged the economy and put many jobs at risk. Family life is not all sweetness and light.

Celebrating family life on the feast of the Holy Family, however, is not a matter of drifting into sentimentality. The readings from the Gospel that are read in church on this day, whichever Sunday it may be in the three-year cycle of readings, all highlight crises. The first relates to what happened after the visit of the magi, when Joseph is warned in a dream of the threat to the child's life that Herod had put in place. And so the family have to escape to Egypt. The second describes the visit to the Temple and their meeting with Simeon and Anna. Simeon, we are told, believed that he would not die until he had seen the Messiah. He takes the child in his arms and gives thanks to God, declaring, 'Master, now you are dismissing your servant in peace, according to your word.' It is a joyous moment for him. He describes the child as 'destined for the falling and the rising of many in Israel'. The child will bring people to know themselves better, their 'inner thoughts' will be revealed. But he adds a chilling word for Mary: 'a sword will pierce your own soul too' (Luke 2:25–35). What puzzlement or anxiety did that cause the young mother? And the reading for the third Sunday in the cycle is the account of Jesus being lost and found in the Temple in Jerusalem when he was twelve. It is a gritty moment. Here indeed there was puzzlement and anxiety.

Recall the scene. It is Passover and the family has gone up to Jerusalem for the feast. When they set off to return home, Mary and Joseph believe Jesus is travelling in the caravan. We may presume that was what had been planned. But he goes missing. Without a word to them he has decided to remain behind. Only when they look for him towards the end of the first day's journey do they discover he is not there. They go back to Jerusalem and search for him, finding him at last, we are told, after three days. (The number is noteworthy. It is less a measure of time – they may have found him within hours – more a pointer to its significance. How often in the Scriptures decisive moments, and supremely the resurrection, occur on the third day.) They discover him in the Temple, listening to the doctors and asking them questions. What were those doctors making of him?

Mary, however, questions her son: 'My child, why have you done this to us?' Her anxiety is unmistakable. It is not hard to imagine a mother's concern about her missing child. Think of children, like Madeleine McCann, missing more recently in society today.[4] Yet he replies, 'Why were you looking for me?'

4 I think of Deirdre Jacob who was a student at St Mary's University, Twickenham. Her photograph is on the wall of the crypt chapel where I

Was he disappointed that she did not understand him? Did not realise what drove him on? 'Did you not know,' he continues, 'that I must be busy with . . .', busy with what? Translations suggest, 'with my Father's affairs', or 'my Father's business', or 'in my Father's house (understood perhaps as the Temple)'. The expression used is unclear, but most literally it states, 'the things of my Father'. What was the boy saying?

The infancy narratives are complex, as we have already noticed. They reflect with hindsight an emerging understanding of who Jesus is. This episode can be seen as presenting Jesus, even as a child, consumed with a sense of mission, a longing to carry out the will of his heavenly Father. But we may also read it as a moment of crisis between Mary and Joseph and their child.

The Gospel tells us that when Jesus referred to being busy with 'the things of my Father', Mary and Joseph did not understand what he meant. And we may well imagine that the matter was not left there. They would have wanted to know what compelled him to remain behind. Had he perhaps tried to find them, but not succeeded, then stayed because he felt he must? They would have pondered his words. If understanding dawned slowly and even incompletely, they would all the same have begun to glimpse a little more precisely what mattered most to him.

Jesus, Mary and Joseph, now reunited, then return to Nazareth and Jesus lives there 'under their authority', increasing in wisdom as the years passed and in favour with God and those around him. There is calm. The episode in Jerusalem has resolved whatever tension may have existed among them. At the same time, Mary continued to reflect on what has happened, once more treasuring 'all these things in her heart'. She was not brooding, but pondering (Luke 2:41–52).

---

celebrate Mass in the early morning. On 28 July 1998 she went out to post letters and was last seen just a few hundred yards from her home.

In none of these episodes can the family be seen as immune from challenge or crisis, anxiety or puzzlement. Family life is not simple and straightforward, whether for us or for that family settled in Nazareth. We wrestle with complexities, but still, through the maelstrom of complexity, we can see how we are blessed in and by our families. We give thanks and through loving them we bear witness to the gospel. And furthermore, if families offer us one way of bearing witness, our friends offer us another.

St John, the disciple Jesus loved

Two days after Christmas we celebrate the feast of St John, apostle and evangelist. In the Gospel attributed to him, he is never named, but there is reference to 'the disciple Jesus loved'. He sat close to the Lord at the Last Supper, stood by the cross with the mother of Jesus whom the Lord then committed to his care, and, when alerted by Mary Magdalene that Jesus had been raised, ran with Peter to the empty tomb and, when entered the tomb, he believed. For many centuries this unnamed, beloved disciple was identified as John, the son of Zebedee, the apostle and evangelist. Nowadays, however, reputable scholars are not so sure.[5] Be that as it may, what matters here is for us to realise that there was a tradition among the disciples of Jesus that there had been one who was acknowledged as particularly close to him. It can teach us an essential lesson.

If the notion of 'the disciple Jesus loved' takes us aback, it may help to ask whether there were disciples Jesus did not love. To ask the question is to discover the answer. Of course, there were not. How could there have been? At the heart of

5 See Raymond E. Brown, *The Churches the Apostles Left Behind*, (London, Geoffrey Chapman, 1984), p.84, n.120.

the good news proclaimed by Jesus was a gospel of love, the love of God and the love of neighbour. They are not distinct, two separate loves, but two aspects of the same reality. This love is not a matter of mere emotion. It may stir powerful emotion and that can be wonderful. But emotions are mercurial. They pass. This love is based on a surer foundation, not feelings, but a commitment that influences our attitude to every woman and man on this earth. No one is excluded.

However, these fine sentiments are abstract. People who claim to love God by loving everyone, but who actually love no one in particular, are not to be taken seriously. Our loving becomes real through actual relationships. And the mention of one disciple, singled out as special, the disciple Jesus loved, alerts us to the way we make love real.

Some people who love may in fact be rather reclusive. They prefer to keep to themselves. More often, however, when people love deeply, there is something creative about their loving. It reaches out and attracts others to its orbit. It becomes the warm centre of a wide circle. Friends gather and friendships flourish. Many marriages bear witness to that. But the phenomenon is not confined to those who are married. Friendship in its own right has the same effect.

Friends are not absorbed in each other. They share common interests – personal or professional, intellectual or sporting, whatever they may be – with the same enthusiasm. They will talk together and laugh together. They are a guarantee of help to one another, a source of encouragement, and they give comfort and support when life is hard. They will often share a point of view, but at times they may clash. It makes no difference. The bond can cope. It doesn't depend upon perfect agreement. Nor is the circle of friendship closed. Friends are kindred spirits and they welcome others who are like-minded into their company. Friendship is a way of loving that reaches out to include others. It is not preoccupied with sex.

There are those today, of course, who can make no sense of deep relationships, uncluttered by physically sexual activity. They doubt whether they exist. But many of us know better. Happy marriages are often built as much on friendship as on passion and there are many others of us who are single, whether by choice or chance or commitment to celibacy, who delight in our friends. We give thanks for them and, particularly at Christmas, we recognise that they help us make love real. In doing so we keep before us the example, the witness, of Jesus and the disciple he loved.

Witnessing can be expressed in so many ways, such as the courage of Stephen, the complexity of family life, and the commitment of friendship.

★

The Christmas Octave comes to an end on New Year's Day, when we celebrate the feast of Mary, Mother of God. This feast, however, is not to be dismissed as an example of Catholic neurosis, as though after celebrating the birth of Jesus we feel forced to honour his mother as well. Something more profound is being brought before us.

What we need to notice is the Gospel of the day. At Christmas, as I have indicated, the three Gospel passages are focused on proclamation, contemplation, and witness respectively. Few people will attend all three Masses, but many will attend two, usually at midnight and then later in the day. So, while there will be those at the dawn Mass, it will probably be the Mass attended by the fewest people. But on this feast of Mary, Mother of God, the Gospel we hear is the very passage that is proper to the Mass at dawn, where Mary hears what the shepherds have come to tell her and treasures it in her heart.

As the Octave ends, therefore, we find ourselves being invited once more to contemplate the mystery of the incarnation, that God sent his divine Son to be born of a woman, to become truly one of us. The mother of Jesus offers, of course, a pattern for discipleship. She models the witness that those who follow her son are called to bear. She invites us to bear witness. But, confronted by this birth and its bewildering implications, we are also called to treasure the mystery in our hearts and to contemplate.

4

Epiphany: manifestation and mission

Christmas celebrations are not confined to the Christmas Octave and the end of the Christmas season can be marked on different days. First, we speak of the twelve days of Christmas that take us to 6 January, the feast of the Epiphany. On that day, in particular, we reflect on the visit of the three wise men to the newborn child. According to tradition, they come bearing symbolic gifts that identify who he is: gold for a king, frankincense for God, and myrrh, anticipating his death. In some countries, this is when Christmas gifts are exchanged, not on Christmas Day itself. I have memories from the 1960s when I was a student in Rome, of people bringing gifts to policemen on the Epiphany, when they were on point duty, as they were directing traffic. They often brought them panettone.

Epiphany means manifestation. On this day the child who has been born is revealed, made manifest, to the nations. We have noticed earlier that Luke's Gospel principally focuses on the universal vision: the child has been born as the saviour of everyone. Yet in Matthew's Gospel, where the primary emphasis tends to be more exclusively on the fulfilment of the promises made to the chosen people, this universal vision is expressed through the visit of the magi. These three wise men have been seen as representing what were then the three known continents, Africa, Asia, and Europe. What vision could be a more universal than that? And, of course, it is also Matthew's Gospel that will end with the command to 'make disciples of all nations' (Matthew 28:19). There can be secondary as well as principal emphases.

So Christmas and Epiphany may be seen as two sides of the same coin. At Christmas events recounted largely through Luke's eyes: there is the proclamation of the birth of Jesus, the presence of the shepherds who are local people, and that reference to the mother of Jesus, pondering, treasuring in her heart, what she was being told and wondering what it all might mean. The focus is interior, reflective. And at the Epiphany the story is told through Matthew's eyes: the presence of the magi from far-off lands and the gifts they bear that indicate the child's identity. The focus here is external and embraces the whole world. And that large vision is expressed plainly in a passage from St Paul's letter to the Ephesians that is read at Mass on this feast. Paul speaks of the commission he had been given for the Ephesians and declares that this is a mystery, made known to him by revelation. And then he goes on to explain the key feature of this mysterious revelation: what previously has been hidden 'has now been revealed to his holy apostles and prophets by the Spirit: that is, the Gentiles have become fellow heirs, members of the same body, and sharers in the promise in Christ Jesus through the gospel' (see Ephesians 3:2–6).[1] What has been revealed is now recognised as being no longer for the privileged few, but for everyone.

Moreover, the mystery of which Paul speaks, as we have already noticed, is not a puzzle or shallow 'mysteriousness'. What has been revealed refers rather to deep truth. And, as revealed, it implies something that is not of our making – not, in other words, the smart conclusion of human cleverness, but a gift bestowed on us by the Christ-child. However, the very

1 Scholars wonder whether Paul was in fact the writer of this letter, but details of authorship need not distract us. The letter has been recognised as steeped in Pauline thought, so, if Paul was not the author, it must have been written by someone who nevertheless understood his mind intimately.

idea of revelation raises questions because Catholic teaching holds that that revelation came to an end with the death of the last apostle.

*

What was revealed was made known to those who were Jesus' immediate and closest companions, the Twelve. He revealed it to them. Then, once the Lord had risen from the dead and ascended into heaven, once the Word made flesh had departed, there was nothing more to be said. How could there be? The Word made flesh is God's definitive word. But that conviction is hardly straightforward. How can what we believe now, two thousand years later, be simply identical to what those men and women believed long ago? There has been development and when we speak of it with any seriousness, we cannot be referring merely to the way that what had previously been implicit has become explicit. Doesn't development imply something more than that? And if it does, how can it be claimed that revelation ended when the last apostle died? Must not what has come to light since then itself be regarded as something fresh, as new revelation?

These questions have led to much scholarly debate. They need not detain us for long here, but there are two points that are worth noting. First, I find instructive the notion that revelation did not come to an end when Jesus was raised and ascended into heaven, but at the death of the last apostle. Although the Lord is the Word made flesh, his message did not end when he had passed from our midst. To say so points to the fact that what he was revealing was not simply a message, a matter of words, ideas and concepts, but himself, the Word, a person, and so a matter of relationship. Those who had shared that relationship with him, therefore, enjoyed a unique role. He was not just teaching the Twelve lessons, passing on information. Their relationship with him was essential to the revelation, and what that relationship revealed was something they would have gone on discovering for as long as they lived. Revelation is teaching, but teaching rooted in personal relationship.

And the second point concerns the link between revelation and development. If development means that something new has been uncovered, how can that be if revelation, the essential message, came to an end when the last apostle died? Here I find illuminating a distinction made by another Australian Jesuit who is also a friend of mine. Gerald O'Collins has spoken about foundational revelation and dependent revelation. Foundational revelation is the revelation that was indeed given by Christ, his life, death and resurrection, his teaching and the signs he gave, and everything that became known through his relationship with the apostles, while dependent revelation indicates something that is not shackled by a limited notion of development, an exercise in formal logic – the implicit becoming explicit – but acknowledges the way truths, hitherto veiled, come to be recognised among us. They are not simply making explicit what had previously been implicit, but bringing to light here and now something new, but nevertheless dependent upon, embedded in, foundational revelation. What is true profoundly can take us by surprise, open our eyes afresh.[2]

Think of a great play or a piece of classical music. The text of the play is unchanged, the score of the symphony as it has always been, but a gifted director may put on stage a production of the play that reveals depths never imagined before, a gifted conductor may draw from an orchestra an interpretation more breathtaking than any heard before. Here what is already known is giving birth to something new. And when we ask how, we realise that such a play, such a symphony have depths

2 See Gerald O'Collins, *Rethinking Fundamental Theology*, (Oxford, Oxford University Press, 2013), pp. 128–135. In passing we may also notice that O'Collins refers as well to future revelation, what will be revealed at the end of time when the Christ comes again.

to them that have not been realised previously. Gifted produc-
ers or gifted conductors are able to explore those depths and
discover something fresh. This process that unfolds is like
contemplation. It is when we contemplate mystery, deep
truths, that we can find ourselves discovering hidden depths.
What we are discovering is new, but rooted in what we already
knew.

So the feast of the Epiphany, which also celebrates the birth
of the child, invites us in particular to share the good news of
that birth, to make it manifest. Revelation and manifestation
are partners. What was revealed at the birth was made manifest
by the visit of the magi, a manifestation furthermore that
should inspire a sense of mission. But we need also to remember an alternative ending to the Christmas story.

*

After the wise men had left, you will remember that Joseph
learns in a dream, as we heard in Matthew's Gospel, that Jesus'
life was in danger. King Herod felt threatened by the magi's
message that a king had been born, and was determined to find
the child and kill him. Angered that his visitors had not
returned to tell him where he could find the child, he ordered
the slaughter of all the male children under two years old in
Bethlehem and the neighbouring district, a massacre, of course,
that replicates Pharaoh's slaughter of newborn boys at the time
of the birth of Moses. Again, Matthew's Gospel is typically
highlighting fulfilment. Joseph, however, escapes with Mary
and Jesus to Egypt. And when he returns after Herod's death,
he makes his home in Nazareth.

Luke's Gospel, however, knows nothing of this drama. He
tells instead of Mary and Joseph bringing their newborn son to
the Temple, a scene that is sometimes considered on the feast
of the Holy Family, as we have already noticed. But this
episode, too, is not without its drama and is brought before us
again on 2 February, forty days after Christmas, when we

celebrate the feast of the Presentation of the Lord in the Temple, a further ending of the Christmas season.

Mary and Joseph have come in obedience to the law to give thanks for the safe delivery of their child and their visit marks the end of Mary's period of ritual purification following the birth. According to Mosaic law, after forty days a woman had to bring to the priest a lamb as a burnt-offering and a pigeon or turtledove as a sin offering. Mary and Joseph, as poor people, were permitted to bring, instead of a lamb, a second pigeon or a second turtledove (see Luke 2:22–4; Leviticus 12:1–8).

When they come to the Temple, they meet the old man, Simeon, who takes the child in his arms and speaks mysteriously about him. Simeon had lived a devout life, waiting for the one who would bring him salvation. When he saw the child, he believed his wait was over. He could die happily. And so he proclaimed:

Master, now you are dismissing your servant in peace,
according to your word;
for my eyes have seen your salvation,
which you have prepared in the presence of all peoples,
a light for revelation to the Gentiles
and for glory to your people Israel.

Then he speaks to Mary directly, informing her, 'This child is destined for the falling and rising of many in Israel, and to be a sign that will be opposed so that the secret thoughts of many will be revealed – and a sword will pierce your own soul too' (Luke 2:28–35). These words indicate future suffering. Faithful discipleship will never be without its challenges. Let me offer an example.

For me Simeon's words will always be associated with Hugh Campbell-O'Neill. On 15 November 2000, Hugh who was nine-and-a-half years old and whose parents are friends of mine, was cycling to school. He fell off his bike, struck his head, and never regained consciousness. He died six days later. His parents were heartbroken.

Trying to cope, his father clung in part to a prayer that he had first heard on the radio when he was young himself, even before religious faith had meant much to him. The prayer was this very prayer of Simeon's, known from its opening words in Latin as the *Nunc Dimittis*, with its haunting opening line in the King James Version, 'Lord, now lettest thou thy servant depart in peace.' He did not feel Hugh's death had been peaceful at all, nor was he at peace himself.

Between Hugh's death and his funeral, he scarcely slept. One night, while he lay awake, he said this prayer again and then remembered that Hugh had written something about it. The next morning he checked the boy's school RE jotter and found he was right. Six months earlier Hugh had written: 'My favourite story about Mary is the Presentation. When Mary and Joseph take Jesus to the temple and the oldest man ever tells Mary that she and Jesus are going to suffer a lot.' Why will they suffer?

Simeon, as we have seen, goes on to describe Jesus as destined for the falling and rising of many, as a sign that would be opposed, and he refers to the sword that will pierce through Mary's soul. These words are not just a prophecy of Jesus' rejection and Passion or of Mary's grief at the crucifixion of her son. They go deeper. They indicate that this life will reveal people's dispositions. He will be the indicating factor. At a time of crisis, some will accept him, others turn away. Their response will lay bare the thoughts of their hearts, their deepest selves. What matters to them? What matters to us?

The child in Simeon's arms has a message that Simeon, however imperfectly, has discerned. It is a revelation of unlimited loving, a child whose entire life, fired by love without reserve, would bring light and glory. That was the key that would guide him. Our lives rise or fall by the path we follow.

If we follow the child's path, then love without reserve will be our key and bring us too to light and glory. But we must be clear. At times, although acting from the highest motives, the immediate result may still seem disastrous. The warning to Mary is also a warning to us: 'A sword will pierce your soul.' Whatever the tragedy, we must not yield. We hang on with love, not bitterness.

That will not wipe the pain away all at once, but little by little peace will come. Some years after Hugh's death, his father, still scarred by his loss, reflected on Hugh's final unconscious days and his death: 'I daydream that the first person Hugh met after he died was Simeon, and as I look forward to my own death I hope that God's mercy will allow Hugh to meet me and lead me to the light.' We may all hope that those we have loved will rise up to greet us after lives of faithful loving and lead us to that same light.

★

Between the Epiphany and the Presentation of Jesus in the Temple, another feast is celebrated that may also be regarded as a conclusion to the Christmas season. It is the feast of the Lord's baptism. It falls usually on the Sunday following the Epiphany and may help us to understand the way his mission is linked to ours.

It stands to reason, of course, that the baptism of Jesus is not the same as ours. Jesus' baptism by John in the Jordan signals the start of his mission and ministry. It may be understood as a kind of consecration for what was to follow. There are accounts in all four Gospels, but Luke's strikes me as particularly instructive: 'Now when all the people were baptised, and when Jesus also had been baptised and was praying, the heaven was opened, and the Holy Spirit descended upon him in bodily form like a dove. And a voice came from heaven, "You are my Son, the Beloved; with you I am well pleased"' (Luke 3:21–2). Jesus has been baptised and is praying, and there are those references to the Holy Spirit in the form of a dove and the voice from heaven. We need to keep remembering that what is being described is not a verbal photograph; it is not what was seen by those who were present, but it captures what came to be recognised as having taken place. And while our baptism may indeed be different from that of Jesus because he has not been handicapped by sin as we are, yet it is like his in so far as our baptism too is a call to mission and ministry, to a share in his life. For us baptism is a new birth.

In April 2018, I accompanied a group of pilgrims to Rome as chaplain. On the Wednesday we joined thousands of others in St Peter's Square to attend the papal audience and in those days, so soon after Easter, Pope Francis spoke unsurprisingly about our new life in the risen Christ. And during his address he had a request to make of all who were present. He remarked that we probably all knew which day was our birthday, and then he asked, 'But do you know the date of your baptism? Do you know the date of your new birth in Christ?' I had no idea of mine. And his request to everyone, when we had returned to our homes, was to discover that date, to discover when we had been born anew in Christ. And as he finished speaking, he emphasised the point again: 'What is it you have to do when you go home?' So, on my return I did that. I contacted the parish where I had been baptised and was delighted and moved to find that I had been baptised in fact on 6 January 1946, the feast of the Epiphany – the feast that celebrates when the birth of Jesus is made manifest to the nations. What a day for a baptism.

*

Not every Christian tradition, of course, regards infant baptism as so important. In 1990 I attended an ecumenical clergy gathering and our host, a Methodist who had worked in Africa, told with good humour of an occasion when some of the villagers where he was working came to ask him if their children could be baptised. He was taken aback. Infant baptism was not something that he had yet explained to these new adult Christians. He wondered with a laugh whether Catholics had been slipping into the village under a cover of darkness. 'Who told you about children being baptised?' he asked them. 'No one,' they answered. 'But being baptised is such a blessing for us, we want our children to have it too.' Loving parents instinctively want to share good things with their children.

One reason for not baptising the young occurs because there are those who believe that the choice is something to be left until people are old enough to decide for themselves. They see baptising people who are young as depriving them of the opportunity to make their personal commitment to the Lord. Why should Christianity be imposed on them? They should not be programmed in this way. But what is happening when a person is baptised?

Baptism is not a form of programming, but should rather be understood, as I have suggested, as a new birth. That is why Pope Francis was urging those of us who were present at that audience in 2018 to discover the date of our baptism, the date of our birthday as Christians. And this new birth in the Spirit brings about a sharing in the life of Jesus. Moreover, when we wonder about the risk of programming, the image of birth corrects it in two particular ways.

First of all, it is important to remember that from the moment of conception, from the moment every man and woman is conceived, there is something about each one of us that is true and will remain true for all time and for eternity: we are the children of our parents. That truth is unchangeable whether we like it or not. There is nothing we can do about it. And so it is with baptism. As birth establishes a relationship between children and their parents, so baptism, new birth in Christ, establishes a relationship between those who are baptised and Jesus of Nazareth. Once baptised, that relationship can never be undone, any more than a physical birth can be annulled.

Then secondly, although we are unalterably the children of our parents, that fact does not determine the kind of relationship we have with them. We may love them devotedly or loathe and despise them, or we may view them with indifference. Birth does not determine and cannot guarantee how that relationship will develop. And once again, so it is with baptism. The proof is all around us. We see people who have been baptised and who live their lives with delight in accordance with the gospel, but there are many others who have rejected the gospel or become indifferent to it. They have not been conditioned or programmed by the water that was poured over them. Other factors have a part to play. They may have understandably turned their back on the Church because they have been scandalised by the way they have seen Christians behave or the treatment they themselves have received. I knew once of a woman, baptised a Catholic, who was struggling to believe because of the rigid way that she had been taught. It had filled her with guilt and anger. She went to discuss her situation with a wise priest I knew. He asked her a shrewd question: 'Forget about morality,' he said to her. 'If you had complete freedom, what would you like to do?' She answered at once, 'Burn down all the churches.' The way a relationship develops, whether in a family or a faith, depends on much more than the physical fact of birth or baptism. The outcome is never automatic. All relationships, whether social or religious, have to be nurtured with love, if they are to bear fruit. And sometimes it may be, as with that woman, the nurturing may be toxic and cause rejection.

★

Yet something further must be added: Christians do not believe that only those who have been baptised are loved by God. The baptised are not God's favourites, the charmed circle of the beloved elite. Everyone is loved by God. No one is excluded. We only exist because we are loved by God. We have been loved into existence by God. Wonderful as that may be, however, it may also prompt us to ask why, therefore, anyone need bother to be baptised. The answer comes in two parts.

First, there is an incident in Luke's Gospel when John tells Jesus, 'Master, we saw someone casting out demons in your name, and we tried to stop him, because he does not follow with us.' Jesus replies, 'Do not stop him, for whoever is not against you is for you' (Luke 9:49–50). What is significant here is not Jesus' response, but John's reaction. He does not go off in a huff. He is not thinking to himself, 'Well, if all this can be done without putting in so much effort, without traipsing round the countryside with this man, I'll go back to Galilee and get on with my fishing.' The stray follower, casting out demons in Jesus' name, may be a loner, but is doing good. Leave him be. But John stays with Jesus. What a blessing it is to be walking in the master's footsteps, to be close to him as his companion and friend. That is what John's reaction teaches us. There is great goodness outside the Church, but what a blessing it is to be within, attached deeply to the Lord.

Then a second reason for baptising is to receive and respond to God's love in a particular way. In the way Simeon discerned, however imperfectly, when he took the child in his arms; in the way that has been revealed by Jesus himself. It is the way of service and unfailing love for others, especially for those whose needs are greatest. Sharing this life, we are called to spend ourselves in service and love as he did. It is our call to mission.

The ideal is demanding and Christians have often failed in it and fail in it still. But the path of the Nazarene is this path of unreserved love that accepts the consequences of loving whatever they may be, even as he did, even to death. And that death was anticipated in his baptism. It is a reality and a truth we too shall have to confront.

When sinners are baptised, their sins are forgiven. Jesus was without sin. In accepting even John's baptism, however, he began his mission and ministry. He stepped into the place of sinners. He identified himself with them and gave himself to them in love, whatever the consequences might be, even to death – death on the cross. On that cross he bore the weight of human sin and death and conquered. At his baptism, he inaugurated this public ministry. At ours, we are invited to join him in this enterprise.

5

Being ordinary

Christmas and the Epiphany, I have suggested, are two sides of the same coin. Baptism – Jesus' and our own, may perhaps be seen as a third side. If that seems slightly eccentric, a three-sided coin, I'm thinking of the rim as the third side, holding the other two together. So, after celebrating the first two feasts as aspects of the same event, we can regard baptism as a reality that unites us to them. For Jesus, as we have seen, his baptism symbolised his consecration for his mission, and ours sends us out on mission, taking up our share in his.

The next major season in the Church's year is, of course, Lent, but after Christmastide we don't move into it immediately. In fact, we know that, because the date of Easter changes each year, the number of weeks until the start of Lent varies; there may be as few as five or as many as nine. This period is now known as Ordinary Time, a name that may seem drab and colourless. Who wants to be ordinary? But it would be a mistake to be too dismissive. We can value what is ordinary, what is normal. During the imposed lockdown because of the Covid-19 pandemic, when routines were being altered forcibly, how many of us longed for life to become more ordinary again, and we wondered when we would get back to what we regard as normal. We also wondered what the 'new normal', as people called it, would be like.

These ordinary weeks before Lent can be seen as an opportunity to pause. During them we can reflect upon the beginning of Jesus' public ministry. It is not simply a question of filling in time between the dramatic events surrounding his birth, on the one hand, and then his Passion, death, and resurrection, on the other, nor just a matter of spending time becoming better acquainted with his teaching and actions. Beyond that, it is a time where we are becoming acquainted with him.

There was a remark made by Pope Francis at World Youth Day in Rio de Janeiro in 2013 that struck me forcibly. He told those who had gathered: 'Look, read the Beatitudes, which will do you good (Matthew 5:3–11). If you then want to know what you concretely must do, read Matthew 25. That is the model according to which we are judged. With these two things you have an action plan: the Beatitudes and Matthew 25. You don't need to read anything else. I ask you to do this from the bottom of my heart.'[1] I made this point to a group of priests with whom I was working some years ago and one of them then observed that he interpreted the Beatitudes as a pen portrait of Jesus: poor in spirit, mourning with those in sorrow, meek, hungering and thirsting for righteousness, merciful, pure in heart, a peacemaker, persecuted for righteousness' sake. And that persecution for righteousness leads us naturally into the great discourse in Matthew 25 about feeding the hungry, giving drink to the thirsty, welcoming the stranger, clothing the naked, and visiting those who are sick or in prison. His comment was powerful and the Pope's remark telling. This is the Jesus with whom we must become better acquainted.

The different Gospels, as we know, present their accounts of him in their own individual way. They are not like modern biographies. They are teaching documents with their distinctive concerns; what is significant for one may not be relevant for another. All the same, from these different portraits Jesus emerges as a person who is compassionate and merciful and filled with love. When at the end he is led away to be tortured

---

1 See Walter Kasper, *Pope Francis' Revolution of Tenderness and Love*, (New York, Paulist Press 2015), p.34.

and executed, his manner is in tune with what has gone before. Ordinary Time is an opportunity for us to cultivate a disposition, calmly and steadily, so that we may respond wisely when crises arise and in a way that mirrors what we have learnt from him. It is not easy. It takes time. We have to practise. And practice makes me think of my friend, Donald Nicholl, who died in 1997 and who for some years was Rector of the Ecumenical Institute at Tantur, near Bethlehem.

He told the story of being out for a run early one morning during his time at Tantur. On the way back he was running beside a high wall that hid him from anyone lower down on the hillside. At the end he turned to descend the narrow stony track and there, coming towards him, were four Muslim men, walking in single file, on their way to work in the quarry above. He almost collided with them. He could only shout a greeting. But by the time he was passing the fourth of these men, as he said, no more than four or five seconds since he had first appeared, the man had plunged his hand into his lunch bag and taken out a large handful of raisins which he pressed into Donald's hand as he passed, simply saying, 'You are sweating.' Donald was moving too swiftly to shout anything more than 'Thank you.'

What he recognised almost at once, however, was the instinctive generosity of the man. What had happened was too immediate for reflective thought. Relating the incident later to a Muslim friend, he was given a clue to the man's action. 'The man must have been faithful over many years in the practice of his faith,' he was told, 'to have such a pure heart.'[2]

In our world today there can be many reasons to be anxious. We are all aware of the crises, national or international, domestic or social, personal or professional, that can take their toll. The pandemic revealed how easily we can be overwhelmed by

2 Donald Nicholl, *Holiness*, (London, Darton, Longman & Todd, 1981), pp. 149–50.

unpleasant surprises. There is no guarantee against them. But we can prepare. Especially in Ordinary Time, day-by-day, whether personally religious or not, we can practise like that Muslim. We can develop purity of heart, a disposition that is compassionate and merciful, generous and loving. Yet how are we to acquire those qualities?

Ordinary Time recurs later in the year, after the feast of Pentecost. It continues for almost six months, till Advent begins again, and that extended period offers opportunities for reflecting on many aspects of Christian faith and life. But this brief initial period, the few weeks between the Christmas season and the start of Lent, can be seen as a time to prepare ourselves, to attune the heart and the mind to being more Christ-like.

*

Early in John's Gospel there is a scene that can help us. John the Baptist is with two of his followers and, when Jesus passes by, he points him out. 'Look,' he says to them, 'here is the Lamb of God,' and the two of them go after Jesus. It was about four o'clock in the afternoon. They ask him where he lives and he replies, 'Come and see.' They then go with him and we are told that they 'remained with him that day' (John 1:35–9). Nothing further is said. It suggests a period, however brief, of rest, a time of quiet conversation. Who knows what passed between them in those few hours, from late afternoon into the evening? But we need times like that, times for reflection. It is often only when we rest that we are able to see what really matters. It makes sense to find a time to keep silence, to value and protect it.

Of course, there are those who pour scorn on the value of silence. They say it is a luxury they cannot afford, something praised either by those who are privileged or who haven't enough to do. The demands and pressures they face make it entirely impracticable. And there may indeed be some who never have the chance to pause and take stock. That is their misfortune.

On the other hand, however full a schedule may be, it is noticeable that people usually have time for what they really want to do. There are those who are incredibly busy by any standards who still manage, for example, to work out in a gym several times a week or who run daily. It is good to keep physically fit and they may say wisely that they need the exercise to handle the pressure of their busy lives. That may well be true. But we need to be spiritually healthy as well as physically fit. We need periods of silence, time to reflect. Silence may unveil deeper truths. A story I heard some years ago seems to me to illustrate the value of silence, of quiet contemplation.

I was browsing television channels one evening and came across a documentary on Johnny Mercer. Mercer was perhaps the last distinguished contributor to the *Great American Songbook*. At one point the programme talked about Otto Preminger's film, *Laura*, that was released in 1945. When it came out, there was a haunting melody as the theme tune, a melody but no lyrics. Very soon someone suggested that, if there were words, if the melody became a song, it might be a real success. But what made the melody haunting was its unusual structure. It was not easy to find the words to fit the music. It was decided to send the music to Mercer and for about a fortnight he listened to it in his home, playing it over and over again. He let the music seep into him. And then all of a sudden he found that it yielded up the words he was looking for. And a memorable song was born.

What struck me about this story was the way what it described was similar to prayer, but in reverse. When we pray over the Scriptures, we have the words. They may indeed be deeply familiar, but we have read them so often, we may feel they have become stale with nothing more to say to us. We have exhausted them. But that is unlikely. We need to ponder them again and again. Like Johnny Mercer soaking up the melody until it yielded its words, we have to soak up these sacred words, ponder them silently, until they reveal the melody of their mystery. It won't happen all at once and will rarely be the result of detailed analysis. We need to give the process time and must contemplate in silence. Reverent silence is not a luxury. Indeed, the busier we are the more indispensable it becomes. From the silence, wisdom is born.

*

Silence, or at least the opportunity to be silent, was imposed on many people during the Covid-19 pandemic. They had to self-isolate and isolation can be alarming, especially in our western culture that is attuned to constant, immediate, entertaining distractions. In isolation myself, a friend prompted me to think about the Vietnamese Archbishop, Francis Xavier Nguyễn Văn Thuận. I used to see him around the turn of the millennium when I was living in Rome. I heard him speak, but never met him. He was a gentle, distinguished, holy man. In 2001 Pope John Paul II made him a cardinal. He was to die from cancer the following year.

Văn Thuận had been appointed Coadjutor Archbishop of Saigon in 1975, just days before it fell to the North Vietnamese Army, and in August that same year, on the feast of the Assumption, he was arrested and spent the next thirteen years in prison. On his release, he was still held under house arrest until his expulsion from Vietnam in 1991, when he went to Rome. For nine of those thirteen years of imprisonment he was held in solitary confinement. 'Time passes slowly in prison, above all in isolation,' he observed later. 'Imagine a week, one month, two months and more . . . of silence. They are terribly long, and when they become years, they are an eternity.'[3]

People experience events differently, but however severe we may have felt our own isolation to have been, it is unlikely to

3 Francis Xavier Nguyễn Văn Thuận, *Testimony of Hope*, (Boston, Pauline Books & Media, 2000), p.117.

have been as severe as Văn Thuận's. What might he have to teach us? Held in a cell without windows, sometimes the electric light would be left on for days, and then turned off for days, so that he was plunged from constant bright light into total darkness. The stories of his time in prison are legion: how he managed to celebrate Mass each day, how he evangelised to his guards through his friendliness towards them and lack of bitterness, and how he even managed to send people letters to encourage them. But the story that touches me most is his account of his early days in prison, when he felt he was 'suffocating from the heat and humidity to the point of insanity'. And he was distressed because he could not fulfil his priestly ministry. In his eyes, he had abandoned the people of his diocese.

Then one night, as he described it, from the depths of his heart he heard a voice saying to him, 'Why do you torment yourself like this? You must distinguish between God and the works of God.' And he came to recognise that, excellent as his ministry was, his ministry was not God, but God's works, and that God could do things infinitely better than he could, and that he had to choose God alone. He had to hold fast to his choice for God and let God be God. 'This light,' he later wrote, 'gave me a new peace and completely changed my way of thinking. It helped me to surmount moments that were almost physically impossible to overcome. From then on, a new strength filled my heart that stayed with me for thirteen years. Feeling my human weakness, I renewed my choice of God in the face of very difficult situations, and I was never without peace.'[4]

Văn Thuận's trials may be very different from ours, but, if we share his decision to let God be God in our lives, we can develop that purity of heart, that compassionate and merciful, generous and loving disposition that can guide us wisely along our chosen path.

4 Văn Thuận, *Testimony of Hope*, pp.42–3.

These weeks between the Christmas season and the beginning of Lent, therefore, form a kind of interlude – not as a lull, but as an opportunity to know the Lord better. We don't need to be caught up in drama. Rather, day by day we can value what is ordinary and appreciate what can be learnt in silence, especially by easing the pressure on ourselves to succeed, to accomplish our goals. Instead, like Francis Văn Thuận, we can learn to let God be God. And he has another lesson to teach us. We can learn from him to reach out to others. While loving God, we must also love our neighbour as well. This great commandment of love was fundamental for Văn Thuận. No one was excluded, especially not his guards.

He explained that at first the authorities used to change the guards regularly, because they feared, as they put it, that these men would be 'contaminated' by him. Then they stopped the changes, for fear Văn Thuận would contaminate them all. One day one of the guards asked him, 'Do you love us?' 'Yes,' Văn Thuận answered, 'I love you.' The man was not convinced.

'But we have kept you in prison for so many years, without a trial, without a sentence, and you love us? That's impossible!'

'I've been with you many years,' Văn Thuận reminded the guard, 'you've seen it's true.'

'When you are free,' the man asked him, 'won't you send your faithful to burn our homes, to kill our families?'

'No! Even if you want to kill me, I love you.'

'But why?'

'Because Jesus has taught me to love everyone, even my enemies. If I don't, I am no longer worthy to be called a Christian.'[5]

We must love our neighbours. And our neighbours are not just the people we like who live nearby. They can be people with whom we do not agree, or with whom we clash. They

5 Văn Thuận, *Testimony of Hope*, p.70.

may be our fellow Christians. We have a particular opportunity during these early weeks of Ordinary Time to show our love for them.

*

Between 18 and 25 January, there is another Octave, a Week of Prayer for Christian Unity. In John's Gospel, on the night before he died, we recall that Jesus prayed that those who followed him 'may all be one. As you, Father, are in me and I am in you, may they also be in us, so that the world may believe that you have sent me' (John 17:21). These are astonishing words. He was praying that those who were his disciples should be united in a way that reflected his own unity with the Father. What is also remarkable is the fact that this prayer of his has yet to be answered. Even in the earliest days of the Church there was controversy, for example, about whether Gentile converts should also conform to the law of Moses. And other controversies have followed. Then in 1054 there was the Great Schism between Eastern and Western Christianity, and in the sixteenth century, western Christendom itself was torn apart at the Reformation.

However, besides other attempts from time to time, early in the last century and notably since 1908, there were those, especially within the Anglican and Reformed traditions, who longed to achieve Christian unity in a way that would be serious and effective. In pursuit of that aim they worked together and eventually this annual week of prayer for the unity of Christians was established. But in spite of some notable exceptions, Catholics were slower to arrive on the scene. When they finally did so, it was largely through the influence of Pope John XXIII, a person who inspired trust. A commitment to Christian unity was not an option for him. It was integral to his vision for the council that he summoned. The opening sentence of its Decree on Ecumenism declared unambiguously: 'The restoration of unity among all Christians is one of the principal concerns of the second Vatican synod.'[6] And what it has achieved in fact has not been negligible. But neither has it been easy. One image of its struggle is supplied for me, although light heartedly, by thinking of Michael Keegan and Brendan Soane.

*

Michael and Brendan were priests on the staff of the Beda College when I arrived as rector in 1998. When they had a day off, they would sometimes go walking together. One walk to a hill village to the south of Rome was a particular favourite. They would take a bus out of the city and then start their walk. After trekking for hours through the hills they could see the village they were making for close by; it seemed no more than a stone's throw away. By this time, they were also hungry and they always enjoyed a good lunch before returning. But there was a problem. Before reaching the village, which was now so close, they had to make a long, steep descent followed by an equally sharp climb before arriving at their destination. They would describe the experience with wry, good humour, and it seems to me an apt image for our search for Christian unity.

The decision to begin at all may be hard, but once begun, the initial steps can be easy enough, meeting people, liking them, ironing out minor misunderstandings, clarifying positions and discovering that viewpoints that had seemed starkly opposed were not necessarily as contrary as had been imagined. Little by little, real progress is made. Then a major step needs to be taken and we find ourselves, like Brendan and Michael approaching that village, apparently close, but having to descend suddenly and exhaustingly into depths which we had not foreseen, before climbing back to reach the summit. Nevertheless, we must persevere.

There are, of course, those who view this desire for Christian unity with weariness and sometimes with cynicism. 'Why

6 *Unitatis Redintegratio*, Decree on Ecumenism, n.1.

bother? What's the use?' they ask. 'What has it achieved?' And even supposing it achieved complete success, there would no doubt be someone – or some group – the following morning who would be criticising what had been done, complaining about some issue and splintering off. Or even supposing that that did not happen so all divisions between Christians had been overcome perfectly, celebrating this week would still be vital, just as it is vital for us to celebrate important anniversaries, our successes, to remind ourselves why they are important to us. And even now, without achieving the unity for which we long, in spite of obstacles in our way which may seem insuperable, we must continue to build and strengthen our friendships. These relationships form the good soil that in due course will yield a rich harvest. So we must reach out to others. The Week of Prayer for Christian Unity is ideal for that.

★

Each year, a group from a country or culture is asked to supply materials for the Octave to guide prayer and offer a liturgy that can be used when people gather. I have memories that I treasure from my time at the Beda. On the Saturday evening during the week, we would always invite a wide range of friends, Anglicans, Methodists, Waldensians, the Salvation Army and others, to join us for just such an occasion, for prayer and afterwards a festive dinner. Let me describe two occasions. We used the liturgy that had been supplied, but edited it because it tended to be stronger on words than action, and action – some symbolic gesture, was also important.

One year, when, if my memory is correct, the theme was peace and forgiveness, Larry Tongco, who worked in the college as the handyman and could do almost anything, erected an arch out of wire netting in front of the altar. Entering the chapel, the arch was hardly visible, but everyone, as they came in, was given a small olive branch. Then, at the appropriate moment people were invited to come forward, two by two, and thread their branch into that wire netting. By the time a hundred or more people had done this, a bridge had been formed and became visible. It gave simple, but powerful expression to what we were celebrating and to our hope for peace and forgiveness.

On another occasion, the theme was based on the meeting between the two disciples and the risen Christ on the road to Emmaus (Luke 24:13–35). That year we began the liturgy in the common room. After the start which included reading the early part of Luke's text, we processed along the corridor from the common room towards the chapel. We were, so to speak, on the road and we paused on the way, when the next section of the Gospel was read. After that we continued into the chapel. When everyone had found their place, we listened to the concluding section and the service continued.

On this occasion, in front of the altar, Velázquez's painting of the kitchen maid at the supper at Emmaus had been put in place. When Father John Breen, who planned these occasions, had the idea of using it, he contacted the National Gallery of Ireland where Velázquez's painting is displayed. They responded generously and immediately, sending over a copy.

Diego Veláquez, *The Kitchen Maid at Supper at Emmaus*

Beside the picture were tureens from our kitchen, similar to the one in the picture, and they were filled with fruit. Towards the end of the service, when people were invited forward, they were also invited to take a piece of fruit from a tureen, and at the end we processed out of the chapel and down to the refectory where the ceremonial part of the liturgy was concluded. But in a way, of course, it was continued in the festive meal that followed, when the fruit was eaten – and much else besides. These occasions express and build friendship and pave the way for that unity for which the Lord prayed, so that his unanswered prayer may one day remain unanswered no longer.

*

The Week of Prayer for Christian Unity ends, as I have mentioned, on 25 January. It is the feast of the Conversion of St Paul and that initially made it seem an appropriate day to conclude the Octave, a celebration of conversion. But it also fits neatly into this interlude between Christmas and Lent, a period of calm normality, a time for our ordinary routine during which we can pause, value silence, and ponder our identity. Who are we as followers of the Christ? How should we be trying to live? How can our love of God and our love of one another guide us? Those are crucial questions that lead us into the deeper self-knowledge that we need in order for our Christian identity to mature. They help us prepare for Lent.

6

Lent: with Christ in the Wilderness

In 1872 the Russian artist, Ivan Kramskoi, completed his painting entitled, *Christ in the Wilderness*. It now hangs in the National Tretyakov Gallery in Moscow. Jesus is seen sitting on a pile of small rocks. Edward Elgar had a copy in front of him when he was composing his oratorio for Newman's *The Dream of Gerontius*, and I have had a copy in my study for many years.

Ivan Kramskoi, *Christ in the Wilderness*

Sometimes, when I look at it, Jesus just seems exhausted, as though saying to himself, 'How ever did I get myself into this mess?' Yet at other times his gaze seems to be contemplative, as though he is lost in prayer. If, during this first brief period of Ordinary Time, we have been trying to become better acquainted with him, now as we move into Lent, we seek to make this relationship deeper than ever. And we accompany him into the wilderness, where he was tempted as he prepared for his ministry.

★

Theologians have sometimes asked whether it was possible for Jesus, the divine Son of God, to be tempted. How could someone who was God have sinned? How can these temptations be real? But the dilemma, however fascinating for those entranced by abstraction, misses the point.

Jesus in the wilderness is described as being tempted in three ways: to turn stones into bread to satisfy his hunger after fasting for forty days, to take a shortcut to power by bowing down and worshipping the devil, and to test the Father by casting himself from the pinnacle of the temple (Luke 4:1–13; Matthew 4:1–11). And these temptations recall the temptations of the chosen people who complained that they were hungry, and God gave them manna from heaven. Then when Moses went up Mount Sinai to receive the Ten Commandments and was gone from them for forty days and forty nights, they lost faith in God and had Aaron fashion a golden calf for them to worship instead. And later in the wilderness when they were overcome with thirst, again their faith in God faltered, until Moses struck the rock and water gushed forth in abundance. The temptations of Jesus, therefore, can be seen as revisiting the temptations of the people of Israel, although there is obviously one vital difference: the people gave in to temptation, but Jesus resisted.

Besides this way of reading Jesus' temptations, however, we may ask whether there is a more personal way of interpreting what happened to him. We do not know precisely, but all three Synoptic Gospels, Matthew, Mark, and Luke, refer to his being tempted. And while Matthew and Luke give virtually parallel accounts of those three temptations, indicative, we may say, of their reflecting on what had happened, Mark, the earliest of the Gospels, is satisfied with a bald reference. After speaking about Jesus' baptism, he writes: 'And the Spirit immediately drove him out into the wilderness. He was in the wilderness for forty days, tempted by Satan; and he was with the wild beasts; and the angels waited on him' (Mark 1:12–13). He adds nothing more. We may then suppose during that time, as Kramskoi's painting can suggest, that Jesus may well have felt tired and become hungry; and, as the enormity of what lay before him began to dawn on him, even though it would not yet have been perfectly clear, he may well have heard and had to wrestle with the siren call to take a different, an easier, path, a shortcut; and even after that he may have wondered in the darkness whether he was right to trust the Father. Had he become confused, deluded? How insidious temptations can be.

I am not suggesting that the Gospels relate precise descriptions of Jesus' experience, but they offer at least a plausible account of the kind of struggle that he faced as he prepared for the ministry to which he was called. It was not going to be easy. And what is essential to understand is that had Jesus given in to temptation, then he could not have been Saviour. To yield to temptation is to undermine identity. That lesson is vital for us. When we give in to temptation, when we do wrong, when we sin, we are lessened, diminished. Jesus resisted temptation, but often we do not. Our Lenten practice should wean us away from sin, strengthen us to resist temptation so as to be the people we are called to be.

*

In Greek the word for sin is hamartia (ἁμαρτία), meaning to miss the mark or to fall short. Another way of describing sin is to see it as a code word for resisting love. Christians believe that creation is a work of God's love, that we, and all that exists, were loved into existence by God. But love and divine love par excellence is never coercive. We are not forced to love God in return. It is possible to resist this love. To resist is certainly to miss the mark, to fall short, to sin. How could that happen? And yet plainly it has.

One explanation points to original sin, the sin of Adam. But this explanation seems shallow when we concentrate on the eating of the forbidden fruit by Adam and Eve in the Garden of Eden. It is more satisfying to take a fuller view by paying attention to four stories that are told in those early chapters of the book of Genesis. There is indeed the disobedience of Adam eating the fruit, but also Cain's murder of his brother Abel, and the corruption that leads to the flood, and the pride that causes people to build the tower of Babel. What we find in these early chapters, in other words, are various attempts to account for human evil. The root cause is identified in turn with disobedience, with violence, with corruption and with pride. What a toxic combination. When people were trying to understand the root of evil, to understand how, having been loved into existence by a loving God, evil could flourish among them, they uncovered an instinct characterised by those features, disobedience, violence, corruption and pride. And so original sin is not to be identified with a single act, but is understood as an instinct brought about by particular behaviours that bring the origin of sinning to birth. This instinct does not taint everything we do, but it is a tendency that we can recognise in ourselves and that we must work to overcome. We miss the mark. We fall short. We sin. We need to repent. Lent, in particular, is a time to repent, to battle against evil. And evil can take a number of forms. It is natural to think of our own mistakes and failings. But first let us look elsewhere. Let us return to Jesus' experience of temptation.

In Luke's Gospel, the account has a chilling conclusion. After Jesus' triumph, we are told that when the devil had finished tempting him, he departed 'until an opportune time' (Luke 4:13). That sinister threat is left hanging in the air. And the opportune time, of course, was to be Jesus' arrest, torture and execution, his Passion and death. As it approached, we read, 'Then Satan entered into Judas called Iscariot, who was one of the twelve', and Judas goes off to carry out Jesus' betrayal (Luke 22:3). Evil had returned to take revenge.

During his torture, Jesus was blindfolded, beaten and mocked. The guards asked him to identify who had struck him. And on the cross he was mocked and scorned by the people and the soldiers, and reviled by one of the criminals crucified with him: if he was the Christ, he should prove it by saving himself. He was despised for his helplessness. But no more on the cross than in the wilderness did he yield to these challenges. Once more Jesus triumphed.

Throughout our own lives, as well, we are engaged in a struggle between good and evil. These two forces are not equal. There is a power in goodness that evil cannot master, but the conflict is not the less real for that. We can discover the cause of evil in people whose lives have been disadvantaged, in those afflicted by psychosis, and in systemic disorder in society. The damage in us can cause us to do damage to others. All the same, although we may do harm through our vulnerability or carelessness or stupidity, the outcome may not have been deliberate and may have involved no malice. But on other occasions we may in fact have acted deliberately, intending to do harm, but we are not, therefore, necessarily beyond forgiveness. According to the old saying, *tout compendre c'est tout pardonner* – to understand everything is to forgive everything.

And yet, to acknowledge the scope of forgiveness should not make us insensitive to the reality of evil. It may be explicable as human error or weakness, we may be its instruments, co-operating all too readily, but sometimes something darker may be at work. There is no need to conjure up a pantomime devil, but, when faced with extreme evil, the lust for power and control, terrorism, the merciless cruelty that delights in genocide, organised crime, human trafficking, the abduction and torture of children, pornography, abuse that may be domestic, physical, mental, or sexual, we need to explore its origin. We have to ask how such horrors could be perpetrated while those involved in these acts are so morally blind that they despise those who protest. What could cause such corruption, such breakdown of the heart?

At times there will indeed be horrors that are explicable: perhaps triggered by mental illness, or some such cruelty inflicted on the perpetrators earlier in their lives; but sometimes the explanation may not be so straightforward. There may also be evil that is the more devastating because it entwines itself around the human heart, anaesthetising or even destroying the capacity for compassion. When extreme evil takes possession of us, corrupting us, breaking down our hearts, it acquires a personal force that is devastating and from which we need redemption.

Pope Francis whom so many admire, has surprised people by speaking quite frequently of the devil, alerting us to evil as personal. It is a way of speaking that can seem quaint or bizarre to modern ears. We are prepared to analyse human weakness and failure, but are sceptical about the devil. Francis, however, as a Jesuit, is drawing on the wisdom of the Jesuits' founder, St Ignatius of Loyola. In the *Spiritual Exercises* that Ignatius composed and from which so many people continue to benefit, he spoke about the clash between Christ and the devil whom he described as 'the deadly enemy of our human nature'. As Michael Ivens, in his outstanding commentary on the *Exercises* has observed, 'Underlying the whole of the *Exercises* is the principle that Christ leads us to a fully human existence, characterised by integration with self and with the world. Satan does the opposite, destroying freedom and if given complete licence, literally death dealing . . . working hiddenly behind a reasonable front.'[1] Besides the wrong that we may commit because of our weaknesses and failure, there is an objective power to be reckoned with that is personal.

*

So Christ in the wilderness was tempted and was bracing himself for the coming struggle. And we with him must discipline ourselves as well. Discipline points us, first of all, to penance. We think of Lent as a penitential season.

In 1970 I came to know Denis Lant in Oxford. Before becoming a Catholic, Denis had been a Baptist minister and every year, for as long as his health would allow, he was invited to preach a sermon at the University Catholic Chaplaincy. They were memorable occasions. One year he preached at the beginning of Lent.

He described Lent as a time for bridging the gap between who we are and the people we know we ought to be. We are called to be people who are generous and prayerful and loving, and we know we fall short of that mark. When we sin, even if only in minor ways, we are falling short, missing the mark. It is not a mere matter of not practising what we preach. It is much more than that. Denis was urging us to live at depth, not superficially. Lent is a time set aside during which, through penance, and also through prayer and the care for those in need, we try to overcome our superficiality, diving deeper and measuring up more perfectly to the reality of what being a Christian means. We are trying to make the surface, what people see, match the deep, our inner reality. I don't suppose Denis would claim he was being particularly original, but I have never forgotten it. Out of the depths we are called to be generous, loving and prayerful. And indeed one way to achieve this is by doing penance.

1 Michael Ivens, *Understanding the Spiritual Exercises*, (Cromwell Press, Gracewing, 1998), pp.106–10.

However, we often tend to shy away from penance, not necessarily because it may be hard, but because it seems negative: giving something up for Lent. All the same, some small daily act of self-denial, something that goes just a little against the grain, precisely because it is small and unspectacular, may reveal to us better than anything else the existence of that gap between who we are and who we ought to be. Perhaps it is not necessary to give up alcohol for Lent; indeed, have some wine with dinner, but can we manage without the gin and tonic beforehand? That may seem too trivial, but small acts of self-denial can help us check reality.

An alternative, of course, is not to give up something we enjoy like alcohol, but to do something positive for others, to care for those in need, which is another of the essential Lenten practices. During the lockdown caused by the pandemic, there were people who showed immense generosity to those who had to isolate themselves. The help they gave to those in need was impressive. After the lockdown, with many people out and about again and able to care for themselves once more, the experience nevertheless revealed that there are others who remain housebound more permanently, living largely on their own. Are they now being left isolated because the crisis has passed? Who are the people who still need our help? Our Lenten service may be to visit them or shop for them. Are we apprehensive in case what we begin for the weeks of Lent may become a longer, more demanding commitment? And yet it may be that our Lenten practice should shape our lives profoundly, not merely as a feature of these few weeks each year. Lent is a time for penance and for service as well.

*

In the garden before his arrest, Jesus roused his dozing disciples and asked them, 'Could you not stay awake with me one hour?' (Matthew 26:40). During Lent, besides penance and the care of those in need, we are also summoned to prayer. Kramskoi's *Christ in the Wilderness*, I have suggested, sometimes seems exhausted and anxious, but I can also see him as absorbed in prayer.

We often confess that we are no good at praying, and we would be wise to be suspicious of anyone who claimed to be an expert. But while we should not become conceited, it is good as well not to be too hard on ourselves. After all, in what do we suppose 'good prayer' consists? Is it a combination of lofty ideas, expressed in eloquent words, that fill us with a sense of overwhelming consolation? Well, there may be moments like that, when the ideas and the words that express them and the emotion that accompanies them seem to buoy us up. But, certainly in my experience, they will be rare. And, should we experience such moments, we shouldn't imagine we are taking the Lord God Almighty by surprise. God has heard it all before.

A favourite guide of mine in prayer is Sister Wendy Beckett. We met only once, briefly and in surprising circumstances. In 1995 we both found ourselves attending a Mass celebrated by Pope John Paul II in his private chapel in the Vatican. After the Mass, before the Pope came to greet those who had been present, I took the opportunity to speak to her and thank her for a short article she had written many years before for a periodical that was then called *The Clergy Review* (now *The Pastoral Review*). She had called the article 'Simple Prayer' and it is a gem.[2] She told me that it was the only time she had ever been asked to write such a piece, although since then she has written on prayer more fully, notably in a book published in 2006.[3]

In that short article, Sister Wendy describes the essential act of prayer as standing 'unprotected before God'. What then will

2 Wendy Mary Beckett, 'Simple Prayer', *The Clergy Review* lxiii, (February 1978), pp.442–5.
3 Wendy Beckett, *Sister Wendy on Prayer*, (London, Bloomsbury, 2006).

God do? She answers, 'He will take possession of us.' To say, therefore, that prayer is simple does not mean it is easy; we may find it very difficult, but it is not complex. 'Prayer is prayer,' she writes, 'if we want it to be.' The key is desire. What do we truly long for? She continues, 'Ask yourself. What do I really want when I pray? Do you want to be possessed by God? Or, to put the question more honestly, do you want to want it?' It is a humane question. Challenged by it, forced to say whether or not we want to be possessed by God, many of us may reply, perhaps shamefacedly, that we aren't quite sure – perhaps we don't, but, we might acknowledge, we wish we did. And that is enough. 'Do you want to want it?' she asks.

> Then you have it . . . When you set yourself down to pray, *what do you want*? If you want God to take possession of you, then you are praying. That is all prayer is. There are no secrets, no shortcuts, no methods. Prayer is the utterly ruthless test of your sincerity. It is the one place in all the world where there is nowhere to hide.[4]

When we pray with renewed commitment in Lent, as we accompany Jesus into the wilderness, what do we want? Do we want God to take possession of us? Then God will. Prayer is simple, not because it is easy, but because it isn't complicated.

Michael Hollings, truly a man of prayer, coined the phrase, 'Prayer is addictive, but the hangover comes first.' I think he was speaking from experience. As a young man he had been an officer in the Coldstream Guards during the Second World War. He was seriously wounded in December 1942 and was awarded the Military Cross for his 'devotion to duty', his steadfast leadership, in spite of his injury. He left the Army in 1946 and decided to test his vocation for priesthood because he wanted to help people. He was sent to the Beda College in

4 Beckett, 'Simple Prayer', p.443.

Rome. The change for him was dramatic. As he was to explain later, 'After being a Company Commander in a Guards Regiment with respect, power, authority and responsibility, I found it very hard to be nobody, with nothing.'[5] One way in which he coped was by discovering a pattern of prayerfulness.

In the afternoons in Rome, instead of taking a siesta, he would go out, especially to the church of San Claudio in the Piazza San Silvestro, near the English Church, where there was exposition of the Blessed Sacrament. 'There,' he has written, 'I often literally sweated it out, in a dull, dumb, boring, knee-aching slog. I slept there often. I seldom had much sense of prayer. Yet I went back there again and again, day by day, like a drowning man grabbing at a lifeline.'[6]

Prayer, though simple, may not be easy, but it is also addictive. However, unlike other addictions, such as alcohol, drugs, or gambling, the hangover comes first. We may resist initially, feeling dull, dumb, and bored like Michael, but if we persevere and overcome the hangover, we find ourselves going back again and again, grabbing for the lifeline that transforms and blesses everything we do, even in our bleakest moments.

★

One other obstacle to prayer seems worth mentioning. It may arise from temperament. What I have been outlining seems to be more accessible for those who are introverts. When people speak or write about prayer, they will often bring out the importance of giving time to prayer, drawing attention, for example, to Jesus' words, as I have done, 'Could you not stay awake with me one hour?' Prayer needs time, and also silence. While those whose personalities are more introverted may be more readily at ease with those conditions, for extroverts

5 Michael Hollings, *Living Priesthood*, (Great Wakering, Mayhew-McCrimmon, 1977), p.20.
6 Hollings, *Living Priesthood*, p.21.

lengthy silence in solitude for prayer may be a real burden. Of course, no healthy person is exclusively introvert or extrovert, but there are those who are distinctly more one than the other. Is prayer then an activity more suited to introverts? That cannot be true. Prayer is for everyone. But, in the well-known advice of Abbot John Chapman of Downside, you must 'pray as you can, not as you can't'.[7] How then do extroverts pray? It is a question that has intrigued me for a long time. Let me try to respond by offering two examples.

Cardinal Cormac Murphy-O'Connor died in September 2017. He was certainly a prayerful man and he was also one of the most sociable people you could ever hope to meet. He loved a party and was wonderful company with a fund of stories that lost nothing by repetition. The evening before his requiem Mass, Solemn Vespers were sung in Westminster Cathedral and Archbishop Bernard Longley of Birmingham preached. He reflected on the Cardinal's motto, *Gaudium et Spes*, Joy and Hope, drawing attention to hope as the source of his joy. Cardinal Cormac's hopefulness, the Archbishop remarked, made him rejoice at the potential he saw in others: 'He could often see the potential for good that others failed to recognise in themselves.' And so he encouraged a whole range of people 'to take up tasks which they never imagined or believed themselves capable of fulfilling'.

For me, listening to those words helped me to understand something about the way extroverts pray. A prayerful and reflective man, Cardinal Cormac nevertheless had a strong extrovert side to him. And a key feature of his prayerfulness was his capacity to see good in others and reach out to them, encouraging them to fulfil their potential. Isn't that at least a clue to how extroverts pray, revealed by their ability to recognise other people's potential for good and their giftedness, encouraging it and rejoicing?

7 John Chapman, *Spiritual Letters*, (London, Sheed and Ward, 1935), p.109.

My other example is of my dear friend, Mary David Totah. She had died just three days before Cormac. She was, of course, an enclosed nun who has also written illuminatingly about the history of enclosure.[8] She was obviously committed to solitude and silence. But she too had a vivid extrovert streak to her as well. In the customary address to the community after her death, the abbess spoke of the encouragement that Mary David had given to young people and notably to the novices during her many years as novice mistress, and she declared: 'With all the warmth of the extrovert, [Mary David] saw easily the good in each one, admired it genuinely and brought it to light with great charity.' Her words seem to echo what Archbishop Bernard had said about Cormac. Prayerful extroverts are alert to the goodness in others and help them develop their giftedness.

★

Renewing our commitment to being prayerful is integral to our Lenten practice. But still prayer can disappoint us. Jesus said, 'Ask and it will be given you' (Matthew 7:7). But how often do we ask without receiving an answer. What sense then can we make of unanswered prayer? And there is a line in the Letter of James, as translated in the Jerusalem Bible, that seems to make matters worse. It can read like a smack across the face: 'Why you don't have what you want is because you don't pray for it; when you do pray and don't get it, it is because you have not prayed properly' (James 4:3).[9] Is that really so?

I received a letter some years ago from an American friend of mine. It was a long time since I had heard from her, although

8 Mary David Totah, 'The History of Enclosure', in Dom Jean Prou, OSB, and the Benedictine Nuns of the Solesmes Congregation, *Walled about with God*, (Leominster, Gracewing, 2005), pp.25–108.
9 The NRSV version states, 'You ask and do not receive because you ask wrongly.'

her husband had kept me abreast of their news. In 1988 she was in a car accident and since then has never been free of pain, intense and focused, accompanied by flu-like aches and fever. She has fought against it, but nothing has helped. Now she is being told that she has an auto-immune disease that is not yet identifiable.

In her letter she writes, 'I just don't know what to pray for anymore. It seems none of my prayers have been heard, much less answered . . . Spiritually, I feel little but emptiness. I've tried to keep my faith, but I can find no solace in it, no joy in it.' She continues, 'In an effort to understand and accept this suffering, I've begged God to show me why this is happening, not just to me, but to my family. I beg for a way to overcome this condition, or at least cope with it better.' And she adds, 'I keep thinking about God's reassurance that he will allow no more suffering than we can stand, but I have to say that I don't much believe that encouragement anymore.' Is she not getting what she wants because she isn't praying properly? And when we pray in times of crisis to avert disaster and our prayer goes unanswered, is it our fault?

We must be fair to St James. He was not laying down some general principle but rather calling to order people who had become slack and thought they could use prayer as a quick fix for their shallow desires. Their prayers went unanswered because they weren't serious. But is there any help or hope that can be offered to those like my friend whose honest prayers go unanswered?

No glib reply will do, but perhaps we need not be completely at a loss. And one clue to a response may indeed be found in her letter (which I am using with her permission). She begins like this: 'I'm almost ashamed to write after so long, but I've decided I must pull myself out of my self-imposed isolation. Contacting old friends is my best first step.' So often, when afflicted by pain, crisis, or tragedy, we do what she had done: we turn in on ourselves. Our suffering absorbs us which is entirely understandable. But, if that attitude prevails, it can lead to a kind of entombment. We become buried, sinking into a sort of grave. Somehow, although it may take a long time, that attitude must be overcome. Like my friend, we have to shift our disposition and break free from self-imposed isolation.

When we do so, we may begin to discover – not perhaps the answer we had expected – but one of another kind. Close to where I used to live in Rome there is a dramatic symbol of such a lesson: the monastery at *Tre Fontane*, the Three Fountains, is believed to be the site where St Paul was put to death. The place acquired its name because, according to legend, when Paul was martyred, his severed head bounced, striking the ground three times, and from each spot a spring of water sprang – and so the three fountains.

Whatever we may think of the legend, the lesson is full of power: there are no wounds, however incurable they may seem, that cannot become fountains, sources of new life. To acknowledge that truth and cling to it is not like a balm, soothing and eliminating suffering. If only it could. But it can draw the sting. We may still feel the pain, but it need no longer enslave us. We are no longer its victims. Little by little, as our disposition shifts, our wounds become fountains. We realise we have not been abandoned and so we find, not perhaps the answer we had hoped for, but a way forward that can still refresh and renew us. It is the very essence of Lent, drawing us on from death to new life.

7

Transfigured in Lent

On 6 August many Christians celebrate the feast of the Transfiguration. It marks the occasion when Jesus went up a mountain to pray, taking with him just three of his disciples: Peter, James and John. And then something happened. Once again, what actually took place, we don't know, but all the accounts in three Gospels speak of their seeing Jesus transfigured, his face shining, his clothes becoming dazzlingly white, and Moses and Elijah appearing with him: Moses, the lawgiver, who encountered God on Mount Sinai and received the Ten Commandments (Exodus 20:1–17), and Elijah, the great prophet, who met God on Mount Horeb in the still, small voice (1 Kings 19:8–12 RSV).[1] The vision is understood to imply the fulfilment in Jesus of the Law and the Prophets. Then a cloud overshadowed them and the disciples heard a voice from the cloud, speaking of Jesus as the Beloved, the Chosen, and commanding them to listen to him. They were terrified. Peter burbles something about building dwellings for Jesus and Moses and Elijah. But when they look up, they find no one there, only Jesus, and he instructs them to tell no one what they had seen (Matthew 17:1–8; Mark 9:2–8; Luke 9:28–36).

What is celebrated in August, however, is also recalled each year on the second Sunday of Lent. In a sermon that is part of

[1] The NRSV translates the more poetic phrase as 'the sound of sheer silence'.

the Office of Readings in the Divine Office for this day, Pope Leo the Great who was Pope from 440 to 461, offered an explanation for Jesus' Transfiguration. He declared: 'By changing his appearance in this way he chiefly wished to prevent his disciples from feeling scandalised in their hearts by the cross. He did not want the disgrace of the Passion, which he freely accepted, to break their faith. This is why he revealed to them the excellence of his hidden dignity.'[2] However, if Leo was right about the purpose of the Transfiguration, then we would have to conclude that Jesus was singularly unsuccessful. His plan fell apart. At his Passion, the disciples were scandalised and terrified, and they abandond him.

The Jesus whom we contemplate in glory in August we see rather differently during Lent. These first two Sundays may be viewed as twinned and they have something to teach us. They reveal who Jesus is. First of all, in the wilderness, tempted and under pressure, Jesus was vulnerable and apprehensive; then, on the mountain, transfigured in the presence of Moses and Elijah, while the voice from the cloud proclaims him as Beloved and Chosen, Jesus was seen in glory. In both events, whether tempted or transfigured, Jesus is revealed as the one who is perfectly faithful. Jesus being tempted is overshadowed by darkness; Jesus transfigured is bathed in radiant light. Both resisting temptation, in spite of vulnerability, and the Transfiguration point to fulfilment that is realised through fidelity.

To follow Jesus is to want to be as faithful as he was faithful. Fidelity in love, whatever the consequences, lies at the very heart of Christian discipleship. And Lent in particular, as we have already considered, is the time when by penance and the service of others and by prayer Christians seek to be formed more securely in that fidelity. To remain faithful under pressure is at first the way of the cross, the way to death. That cannot be

2 Pope St Leo the Great, Sermon 51, *The Divine Office* ii, (London, Collins, 1974), p.120.

avoided. But fidelity is also ultimately the way to resurrection. As we continue through Lent, we may begin to see ways in which, even in the middle of our daily struggle, we are being called to be transfigured.

*

The Lenten season is punctuated by Gospel passages that refer to penance and new life, such as Jesus cleansing the temple as his ministry begins (John 2:13–22), his telling the parable of the prodigal son (Luke 15:11–32), and his forgiving the woman who had been caught committing adultery (John 8:2–11). But, after reflecting on Jesus being tempted and transfigured, and before we come to Passiontide, the backbone of the season may be found in three key episodes from the fourth Gospel: Jesus meeting the Samaritan woman by Jacob's well, his healing of the man born blind, and his raising to life his friend, Lazarus, who had died. They are the focal points of the third, fourth, and fifth Sundays of Lent respectively in the first year of the three-year cycle of readings, but they can be used in fact every year. And they give us clear guidance through the middle period of the season.

The Samaritan woman at Jacob's well

Jesus meeting the Samaritan woman at Jacob's well is one of the great set pieces in the first part of John's Gospel (John 4:5–42). Jesus is sitting, tired and alone. His disciples have gone off in search of food. The woman comes to draw water and Jesus asks her for a drink. She is startled that a man on his own would address her – and even more surprised because he is a Jew, she a Samaritan, and Jews did not associate with Samaritans. So a conversation begins.

They talk about the water that people drink from the well – water which, however good, will soon leave them thirsty again. Jesus indicates to her another kind of water that satisfies thirst utterly and which he can offer: 'those who drink of the water that I will give them,' he tells her, 'will never be thirsty again.' He describes it as a spring inside a person, 'gushing up to eternal life'. The woman is naturally eager to receive this water so as not to have to come to the well again, but, of course, she does not yet understand the kind of water of which Jesus is speaking. And so their conversation continues.

Reading this scene always reminds me of my friend, Damian Lundy. Damian was a De La Salle Brother who died far too young, at aged fifty-three in 1997. He was a lovable man, enormous fun to be with, an inspirational teacher, creative, imaginative, and prayerful, and someone whose influence for good in many people's lives has been inestimable. I think of him now because of a short meditative piece he once wrote about wells and water, prompted by this meeting between Jesus and the woman.[3] The water Jesus offers is, of course, the gift of gospel life. As gift, it isn't of our making. As gift, it comes to us freely and we are meant to take care of it. As Damian remarked, we are its guardians, not so as to keep it from people, but in order to offer it to anyone who thirsts for it. And he goes on to imagine various kinds of people who may come in search of this water.

There are those for whom the water is like an oasis in a desert; they come eagerly because they are tired and thirsty. We should never underestimate people's longing for the divine, for the gift of gospel life. At the same time, what about us? We too may be among those who feel parched and dehydrated, in need of that water.

Then there are others who come happily. They come rejoicing. I recall, for example, a woman in her twenties who was beginning to prepare for baptism, but at that time had

3 Damian Lundy, 'A Journey to the Inner Place', *St Cassian's 1946–1996*, p.12.

little knowledge of Christianity. Her parents had wanted to shield her from religion. One day I remarked in passing, 'You remember the parable of the Prodigal Son.' 'No,' she replied enthusiastically. 'What happened?' It can be easy to forget that there have been these good times, full of joy. And when as a priest I am feeling rather worn down, I have always tried to remind myself of occasions that have gone well, moments for me when priestly ministry has been particularly fulfilling. I think, for instance, of a day in the parish in the mid-seventies when I had to celebrate a requiem Mass and officiate at the burial in the morning for an elderly woman, but then come back to celebrate a wedding early in the afternoon. I have never forgotten that juxtaposition, the sense of privilege I felt at being able to be involved in such crucial events in people's lives. We need to remember the good times. There will be darker moments when everything seems to be fading or falling apart, so these good experiences, etched on the memory, can support us. We probably won't be able to recall how we actually felt. Emotions pass. But we can hold on to the memories and be revived.

Then again there are still others who come who are neither eager nor happy. If they can manage to come at all, they drag themselves painfully and hesitantly. Damian observed, 'They have been misled in the past, or have lost their way.' That will be the experience of many who have suffered abuse in the Church, whose confidence in a community in which they once had faith, has been undermined. Damian was writing before the more recent scandals became known properly, but his words describe what many may feel: 'Some have drunk bitter waters from poisoned wells or have been let down by old familiar wells which dried up unexpectedly.' And he added, 'No wonder they are disillusioned and suspicious of what they may find there.' Nevertheless, 'they are thirsty', in need of care. It is essential that we care for one another, wearing 'the apron of love'.

A well is not a destination. It is a resting-place on a journey. The water it supplies will be used and so will need to be replaced. 'Above all,' as Damian went on, 'it must be shared with other travellers. If it is not given away, it evaporates.' In the Gospel, the woman shares her experience of meeting Jesus with the townspeople and they then go on to meet him for themselves. They in their turn come to declare their belief in Jesus as the Saviour, not just because of what the woman had told them, but from their own experience. As Damian concluded, 'The more you give away, the more you have and the thirstier you become.'

On our Lenten journey we need to refresh ourselves with living water. The theme is central to the season. At Easter, it is not only the newly baptised who should be converts. Conversion is not a once-in-a-lifetime event. And at the Easter Vigil we hear St Paul reminding us: 'Do you not know that all of us who have been baptised into Christ Jesus were baptised into his death? Therefore we have been buried with him by baptism into death, so that, just as Christ was raised from the dead by the glory of the Father, so we too might walk in newness of life' (Romans 6:3–4). Water revives us. To walk in newness of life is to walk in the light.

The healing of the man born blind

What is light? What is darkness? What is sight? What is blindness? These are the questions that confront us as we move to the second of these three major episodes in the first part of John's Gospel. Jesus heals a man who has been born blind (John 9:1–41).

One day, while they were out walking, Jesus' disciples notice the man and ask Jesus bluntly: 'Rabbi, who sinned, this man or his parents, that he was born blind?' If this question seems like a crude relic from two thousand years ago, we should think again. Whenever I think about this passage, I think also of John Hull. John Hull, who died in 2015, became in due course the Professor of Religious Education at Birmingham University. I did not know him, though I met him once when he came to lecture in the Shrewsbury Diocese while I was the Director of the Diocesan Religious Education Service. He was a Methodist, an impressive man and a gifted speaker. And he was blind. Unlike the man in the Gospel, however, Hull was not born blind, but cataract problems and then detached retinas left him eventually in total darkness.

In one of his books, *In the Beginning There was Darkness: A Blind Person's Conversations with the Bible*, he relates a conversation with a taxi driver who asked him, 'What did you do that God made you blind?' To which he replied, 'Well, nothing more than what most people do, who don't become blind.'[4] And the conversation continued for a little longer. But the point here is the way the taxi driver's question echoes that of the disciples. The link between perceived disability and sin or wrongdoing has not left us. It may even seem to be reinforced by Jesus' criticism of the scribes and Pharisees as blind fools and blind guides (Matthew 23:16,17,19,24,26), although tempered surely by Jesus' words to Thomas, 'Blessed are those who have not seen and yet have come to believe' (John 20:29). And on another occasion, Hull gave a moving account in a letter of the way he understood his condition:

> I do not interpret my blindness as an affliction, but as a strange, dark and mysterious gift from God. Indeed, in many ways it is a gift I would rather not have been given and one that I would not wish my friends or children to have. Nevertheless, it is a kind of gift. I have learnt that since I

4 John M. Hull, *In the Beginning There was Darkness: A Blind Person's Conversations with the Bible*, (London, SCM Press, 2001), p.51.

have passed beyond light and darkness, the image of God
rests upon my blindness.[5]

What an arresting image, his image of God resting on his
blindness. And he refers at once to the line in the hound of
heaven psalm that declares, 'even the darkness is not dark to
you; the night is as bright as the day, for darkness is as light to
you' (Psalm 139:12). God is beyond light and darkness. I
remember reading the text of a lecture given by Archbishop
John Quinn, the distinguished Archbishop of San Francisco
from 1977 to 1995, in which he drew attention to what God
has done in darkness: the Chosen People fled Egypt in darkness and crossed the Red Sea in darkness, Jesus was born in
darkness, died in darkness and rose in darkness, and his tomb
was discovered in darkness. And Quinn concluded: 'God is at
work even in the darkness.'[6]

One valuable response to that question is to be aware that it
is all right not to see clearly all at once. We should rather be
wary of those who feel they have all the answers. I draw
comfort from something taught by St Thomas Aquinas that
Donald Nicholl has pointed out. Aquinas described the beatitude, 'Blessed are those who mourn', as a beatitude especially
for intellectuals.[7] Scholars seek to extend knowledge and
naturally enough they defend what they have discovered. But
later, as their understanding develops, they may realise that
they must take up a new position and abandon what they had
previously cherished. It may feel like a bereavement. To adjust
their way of thinking can bring them real sadness. They mourn.
Who among us can see clearly?

5 Hull, *In the Beginning There was Darkness*, p.48.
6 John R. Quinn, 'Do Not Despair: Christ is present even in darkness',
America Magazine, 3 May 2010.
7 Donald Nicholl, *The Beatitude of Truth: Reflections of a Lifetime*, (London,
Darton, Longman & Todd, 1997), pp.5–6.

And besides times of intellectual darkness, there is spiritual darkness as well, the dark night of the soul about which St John of the Cross has been so eloquent. And it is worth remembering that this darkness is not an experience confined to a few exalted, spiritual individuals. It is much more commonplace. There are those who may find the spiritual life initially taking on fresh depth and importance; it becomes real for them in ways they had never imagined. They feel carried away, filled with enthusiasm. They have never known anything like it. They become convinced that their lives will never be the same again. The experience is like falling in love for the first time. But that degree of emotional intensity does not last. And as it fades, people may feel disappointed and doubt whether their intense experience was genuine. In fact, however, they are being purified – being led from what had been inevitably rather superficial at the start to something much more profound.

And there is a darkness of a different kind. In his small classic, *Simple Prayer*, written in 1984, Jock Dalrymple, a remarkable Edinburgh priest who died the following year, began to describe it: 'We start to wonder if we really believe in God, after all.' He goes on to say that 'Christianity appears to be a fairy tale, with any number of psychological explanations', and adds that we feel we have deceived ourselves about God and about prayer, and that our experiences of religious faith in the past were self-induced. We come to think of the whole 'God business' as a hollow sham. That is how it appears. Faith seems to have been lost. But has it? How might we distinguish between lost faith and this dark night?

Losing faith, I would suggest, is a kind of conversion. It resembles what happened to Saul on the road to Damascus, but in reverse. And if that is true, it should be accompanied by a sense of relief. This kind of conversion, shedding previously held convictions, like any conversion should be experienced as a homecoming, a welcome discovery of how things truly are. There may also be a tinge of regret that earlier familiar certainties have faded, but the regret is tempered by that relief.

The dark night, on the other hand, brings not relief, but desolation. We look out over a bleak, spiritual wasteland. At one level, emotionally and intellectually, everything may seem to have been lost. From this viewpoint, the dark night and lost faith may seem the same. At another level, however, in the very depths of a person's being this darkness heralds a desire beyond emotion, beyond feeling, a desire that perseveres. We are not in denial, nor indulging in wishful thinking. We feel deprived, but challenge the deprivation. And so, in Dalrymple's words, we 'plod on, in bewilderment, believing against belief, hoping against hope'.[8]

One person who may illustrate this experience more recently is Mother Teresa, now St Teresa of Kolkata. After her death in 1997, news leaked out of the long years of spiritual darkness that she had suffered and had to endure. Some people even wondered whether she was a fraud. But it was not so. As she once remarked wryly in a letter, 'If I ever become a saint – I will surely be one of "darkness".' But as her friend, Paul Murray, has explained, this was not the darkness of depression or despair; it was rather 'the shadow cast in her soul by the overwhelming light of God's presence: God utterly present and yet utterly hidden. His intimate purifying love experienced as a devastating absence and even, on occasion, as a complete abandonment.'[9] The experience itself must have been terrible at times. Yet, in spite of desolation, a conviction remains that confronts the darkness and waits for the dawn. And in due time the sun rises. Life returns.

8 John Dalrymple, *Simple Prayer*, (London, Darton, Longman & Todd, 1984), pp.97-8.
9 See Paul Murray, *I Loved Jesus in the Night: Teresa of Calcutta, A Secret Revealed*, (London, Darton, Longman and Todd, 2008), pp.18–19.

The raising of Lazarus

In Bethany, a village not far from Jerusalem, two sisters, Martha and Mary, lived with their brother, Lazarus. They and Jesus were friends. When Jesus came to Jerusalem, he would stay with them. They appear most dramatically in the Gospels when Lazarus becomes unwell and dies. But then Jesus visits and raises him from the dead. It is the third of these great set-piece episodes in the fourth Gospel (John 11:1–45).

One notable feature in the account is the way it highlights Jesus' emotions. The fourth Gospel was the last to be written and is generally regarded as the most deliberately reflective of the four, the most theological. On the whole it presents Jesus as reserved and in control. But here, in this episode, there is a difference. When the news of Lazarus' sickness is brought to Jesus, the disciples say, 'Lord, he whom you love is ill.' These words have even led some scholars to wonder, though probably mistakenly, whether Lazarus might not be the man otherwise referred to as the beloved disciple. We are then told plainly that Jesus loved the sisters and Lazarus. And later, when Jesus sees Mary's tears and the tears of those who had come with her, he becomes distressed himself and, when he is taken to the grave of Lazarus, he too weeps. And the bystanders remark, 'See how he loved him.' We are being shown a side of Jesus that previously has been absent in this Gospel.

Against this backdrop what might we learn? As we have noticed already, our tendency these days is to want to know the details of what happened. Had Lazarus actually died and was he brought back to life?

Besides raising Lazarus, there are incidents in other Gospels when Jesus is said to have raised the dead, notably Jairus's daughter (Mark 5:21–43; Matthew 9:18–26; Luke 8:40–56) and the son of the widow of Nain (Luke 7:11–17). We cannot say precisely what happened, but these stories, reported in different Gospels, indicate at least a widespread tradition associated with Jesus' ministry: he brought back to life people who had died.

A notable feature about the raising of Lazarus, however, is the fact that, when Jesus is told that Lazarus is sick, although he loves him, he does not set out at once to see him. He delays. By the time he arrives, Lazarus has been dead for four days. When Jesus asks for the stone to be removed from the tomb, Martha, ever practical, protests, 'Lord, already there is a stench because he has been dead four days.' When Jesus raised Jairus's daughter, he told the mourners that she was not dead, but sleeping. And they laughed at him. Whatever room for doubt there may have been on that occasion, there is no room for doubt here. Lazarus is dead.

The denouement, when it occurs, is stated succinctly. But there have been conversations beforehand. While he is delaying, Jesus tells the disciples that he is glad not to have been there when Lazarus died so that they will believe. And when he reaches Bethany, he speaks first with Martha and then with Mary. They both tell him that, had he been there, Lazarus would not have died. And Jesus replies, 'Those who believe in me, even though they die, will live, and everyone who lives and believes in me will never die.' In other words, the raising of Lazarus is to be believed both as a sign of life beyond death and as revealing Jesus as the source of that life. In one of the most spine-tingling moments in the Gospels, Jesus finally summons his friend, 'Lazarus, here! Come out!' And then he instructs the people, 'Unbind him, let him go free.'

The episode teaches a lesson about faith and eternal life. Lazarus, of course, will die again, as will Jairus's daughter and the son of the widow of Nain. They have been brought back to this life. But when Jesus was crucified and then raised, he was not restored to this life. He was raised to new life. However wonderful life here on earth may be, when it is over, it is not the end. At Easter we celebrate a summons to share new life: unbind them; let them go free.

*

These three Gospel scenes bring into play three powerful images, water, light and life. The water, especially in Lent, reminds us of baptism, but is also to be recognised as a resting place, not a destination. The journey continues. We have to keep moving on, journeying into light. Seeking the light means we travel through darkness as well in order to reach the light and arrive at a new day, which heralds new life, not simply life restored, as it was for Lazarus, but life beyond death, as it was for Jesus. On this journey, receiving refreshing water, travelling through darkness into light, and discovering life renewed offer us, too, transfiguration.

8

Passiontide

On Palm Sunday, at the start of Passiontide, we hear an account of Jesus' Passion according to either Matthew or Mark or Luke. It sets the scene for the coming week. But before that we are reminded of Jesus' triumphal entry into Jerusalem. He comes humbly, riding on a donkey, but acclaimed by his disciples as the prophet from Nazareth, and when his followers are warned by the Pharisees to check their enthusiasm, Jesus answers, 'I tell you, if these were silent, the stones would shout out' (Luke 19:40). This triumph, however, will within days be followed by treachery, torture, and death. We are moving into the climactic events that crown Jesus' ministry. Before we do so, let us pause for perspective.

Working with study groups or with catechists, I have sometimes stated, 'Jesus saved us from our sins by dying on the cross.' The response to the statement, whether spoken or written on a slide or board, is invariably greeted with heads nodding in agreement or a murmur of assent. Then I ask, 'True or false?' The group will look surprised, even alarmed. 'What's he playing at?' they wonder. And I am quick to reassure them that it is, of course, true, but it is also a highly concentrated statement of the truth. It is important to realise that Jesus did not come to die; the purpose of the incarnation was not to bring about the barbarism of death by crucifixion. Jesus came, not to die, but to reveal the Father's love for us, a love without reserve.

To put it rather trivially, we do not believe that, because he was divine, Jesus could just have appeared on earth on the

Thursday, as indeed a true human being, been arrested that evening, interrogated and tortured overnight, and executed the following day, and that would have been human salvation, all done and dusted. We are not saved by a gruesome crucifixion. There is, it is true, a theology of the cross that speaks of it as the infinite price to be paid for humanity's infinite wrongdoing, the sin of Adam. Finite, sinful humanity could never offer the infinite recompense that was in justice owed for the infinite wrong done to Almighty God. Only Jesus himself, truly human, was able to offer infinite recompense on our behalf, because, although truly human, he was also truly divine and so was able to offer the infinite compensation that otherwise was beyond human reach. The approach has a history and a neat logic to it, although its image of God the Father, sulky and petulant and demanding, so to speak, his pound of flesh before welcoming humanity back into his good graces, leaves rather a lot to be desired. It won't do. Instead, love is the key.

Fundamental to Christian faith is the conviction that the whole of creation is a work of divine love and that God created all of us, men and women, out of love. But this love is not coercive. True love never is. And so we could resist it, as we did. As we noticed earlier, resistance to God's love is one way of describing sin. But God's love is inexhaustible. In spite of our resistance, God invites us back in so many ways and the supreme invitation is realised in Jesus. He came, was born, lived, ministered, taught and healed, suffered and died, and was then raised from the dead, in order to reveal the Father's unlimited love for us. Sometimes, when I have written or spoken about these things, people have accused me of diminishing the significance of the cross. But that could not be further from what I am saying.

To speak of the Father's *unlimited* love is to speak of a measurement, a love without limit. How can we conceivably measure love? But, I would suggest, there is a way. We can measure love by its consequences. How much do you love a person? It is possible to give an answer by asking, how much will you do for him or her? How much will we do for a member of our family or a dear friend? More, probably, than we would for a casual acquaintance or a stranger we happen to pass in the street. But Jesus came to reveal the Father's love for all of us. Jesus is our brother. There is nothing he will not do for every one of us, even to accepting death – death on a cross. So the cross is not diminished, but stands at the very heart of Christian faith as the unassailable symbol of God's unwavering, unfailing love for us. And it is the revelation of that love that is contemplated, commemorated and celebrated during Passiontide, especially during the Sacred Triduum: Maundy Thursday, Good Friday and Holy Saturday.

The liturgy of the Triduum is continuous. The Mass begins on Maundy Thursday evening with the Mass of the Lord's Supper, but it does not end with a blessing, as is customary. Rather, there is a procession to an altar of repose where the Blessed Sacrament, consecrated during the Mass, is reserved for distribution at the afternoon liturgy on Good Friday, the Commemoration of the Lord's Passion, which itself begins without formal introduction and ends without a blessing. On the following evening, after the blessing of the fire and the lighting of the paschal candle outside, there is a procession into the church where the Lord's resurrection is proclaimed, a series of scriptural readings are heard that move those who have gathered into the celebration of Mass which includes the blessing of water and the renewal of baptismal promises as well as the baptising of catechumens and the reception of others who seek full communion with the Catholic Church. Then the eucharistic liturgy follows and this extended liturgy ends at last with a blessing and sung alleluias. This liturgy is a powerful experience and many themes are woven into it. I am less concerned here with the liturgy as such and more with some of those themes.

*

Maundy Thursday

On Maundy Thursday, the Mass of the Lord's Supper has a triple focus: the institution of the Eucharist, the institution of ordained priestly ministry, and the fulfilment of the great commandment of love. And these three themes are evidently intertwined. The Eucharist takes centre stage. Even Christian traditions that place less emphasis on sacraments will speak of Jesus as affirming the essential importance of baptism, notably at the end of Matthew's Gospel, when he told his eleven remaining disciples to go and make disciples of all nations, 'baptising them in the name of the Father and of the Son and of the Holy Spirit' (Matthew 28:19), and of instituting the Eucharist at the Last Supper. And because of this emphasis on the Eucharist at the Supper, it has become traditional to speak of ministerial priesthood being instituted at the same time.

The emergence of ministerial priesthood, however, took place over many years, even centuries. Very soon in the life of the Christian community, the responsibilities laid on the Twelve came to be shared. The loss of Judas, his betrayal and death, led to a replacement for him being found almost immediately, and Matthias was elected so that the eleven could become the Twelve again (Acts 1:15–26). Some time later, deacons were appointed to assist in the apostles' ministry, and in due course we find Paul, for example, appointing people like Timothy and Titus and giving them responsibility for communities he had established. But a more formal recognition of ministerial priesthood, of the Sacrament of Order, took a long time to emerge and continues to this day. We have only to think about the debate surrounding the ordination of women. There is not space here to relate that lengthy process of development, but let me offer a brief, though inevitably inadequate, sketch.

Almost from the start, three vital functions of priestly ministry can be discerned. First, there was the proclamation of the

Gospel, the preaching of the Word. Secondly, what was proclaimed was celebrated in worship, especially through the sacraments, people were baptised and bread was broken. And thirdly, what was proclaimed and celebrated was made real, realised, in service, normally expressed through leadership. The three elements – Word, sacrament, and service – have been constant features of priestly ministry, but over the centuries the emphasis has shifted, their individual prominence has varied.

When trying to gather an understanding of the emergence of priestly ministry, therefore, it is helpful to recognise that initially it was the preaching of the Word that had pride of place. The disciples went out to preach the Word, to proclaim the good news of Jesus Christ. In time, that gave way to the element of service, expressed as leadership, being given priority. What events caused such a shift? The growth of the Christian community, the spread of the Church and its sheer size, meant there was a need for organisation. Then, in time of persecution, and later of respectability, when Christianity was accepted as the religion of the Roman Empire, organisation was also essential. In due course, however, that gave way to an emphasis being placed on cultic power: first, in order to salvage the Church following the collapse of the Roman Empire, then to frustrate the ambitions of secular rulers, and finally to resist the protests of the sixteenth-century Reformers.[1]

At this stage, not least through the spread of monastic life which had a strong missionary bent – think of Gregory the Great sending Augustine of Canterbury to England – the service of the body of Christ shifted in meaning from the

1 See Paul Bernier, *Ministry in the Church: A Historical and Pastoral Approach*, (Connecticut, Twenty-Third Publications, 1992); Roderick Strange, *The Risk of Discipleship: The Catholic Priest Today*, (London, Darton, Longman & Todd, 2004), pp.38–44.

service of the people as Christ's body to care for the sacramental body of Christ in worship. Over two thousand years, different elements have had their day claiming prominence. What is amazing is to realise that perhaps never until our own time has a deliberate attempt been made to put together an integrated understanding of priestly ministry: the Word that is proclaimed is celebrated in sacrament and made real in service. That is the vision set before us by the Second Vatican Council.

★

A second theme, and central to our celebration of the Mass of the Last Supper, is the institution of the Eucharist. During the Mass, we listen to the account of the Last Supper that Paul sent to the Corinthians. It is the earliest account we have, earlier than those given in the Gospels. Paul wrote:

> For I received from the Lord what I also handed on to you, that the Lord Jesus on the night when he was betrayed took a loaf of bread, and when he had given thanks, he broke it and said, 'This is my body that is for you. Do this in remembrance of me.' In the same way he took the cup also, after supper, saying, 'This cup is the new covenant in my blood. Do this, as often as you drink it, in remembrance of me.' For as often as you eat this bread and drink this cup, you proclaim the Lord's death until he comes (1 Corinthians 11:23–6).

Dates are difficult to determine. Let us suppose, as people have sometimes suggested, that Jesus was born in fact around 6 BC. If the supper was taking place when he was a little over thirty years old, perhaps, therefore, in AD 28, and Paul was writing this letter to the Corinthians, as is generally agreed, around AD 58, then Paul was writing just about thirty years after the event. Two points are striking.

First, notice Paul's opening words: 'I received from the Lord what I also handed on to you.' Paul has actually been criticising the Corinthians for their selfishness when they gather, as the wealthy were tucking into the food while the poor were going hungry. But in correcting them, he's not saying, 'Here's a bright idea I've had. Why not think of your gathering in this way and treating one another better?' No. He tells them, 'I received from the Lord what I handed on to you.' So it is not his bright idea that he is appealing to, but within thirty years an established tradition. There was no internet, no Facebook, no instant communication, yet within that brief period of time a tradition had been established that Paul could appeal to with confidence. And second, describing the Lord's Supper, Paul uses the verbs that have remained at the heart of every authentic Eucharist: Jesus took bread, gave thanks (that is, in Greek, made Eucharist of it, or blessed it), and broke it, before handing it to his companions; taking, blessing, breaking, and giving. So early on, a tradition was established.

I wonder how the Twelve reacted, how they felt. They had come to celebrate Passover and suddenly, when taking the bread and taking the cup, before handing them to his friends as was customary at the Passover meal, Jesus paused and identified himself with the elements. 'This is my body. This is the new covenant in my blood.' How bewildered they must have been. How could they make sense of it? It was not until later, after watching fearfully and shamefacedly from a distance as Jesus died on the cross, and then as they welcomed the risen Christ with joy, that the disciples came to recognise what they had been taking part in, what they had been celebrating; it was a different Passover, not from physical slavery to freedom, but from death to new life.

*

The Gospel we hear at the Mass of the Last Supper is from the fourth Gospel. There St John gives no account of the institution of the Eucharist, but describes instead Jesus washing the feet of his disciples. There is more bewilderment and Peter protests at the attempt to wash his feet. But Jesus tells him that if he doesn't then Peter can have nothing in common with him; Peter, at once and typically, swings to the other extreme, offering not only his feet but his hands and head to be washed as well. Jesus tells him, I imagine with dry, patient good humour, that for his feet to be bathed is quite enough. And then he teaches them all that, as he, the Master, has served them washing their feet, so they should serve one another. Indeed, what has been celebrated in Eucharist is to be expressed in service. During the Mass, after preaching, the priest washes the feet of some of those with him.

*

Good Friday

One Wednesday in Oxford during Holy Week, I said to Denis Lant, 'I'll see you on Friday, Denis.' He was becoming too old to come out on the Thursday evening, but I took it for granted he'd be there on Good Friday for the Commemoration of the Lord's Passion. 'No, you won't, mate,' he replied firmly, and explained that he always remained at home on Good Friday, in mourning. I have never forgotten it.

As I contemplate the Passion I find it helpful to view Jesus' seven words from the cross in chronological order. They have often been used as a prompt for prayer. In the earliest account of his crucifixion that is supplied by the tradition common to Matthew and Mark, Jesus speaks from the cross only once. It can be heard as a cry of anguish and desolation: 'My God, my God, why have you forsaken me?' (Matthew 27:46; Mark 15:34). In Luke's Gospel, he speaks three times. They are words of compassion. He prays for those putting him to death: 'Father, forgive them, for they do not know what they are doing.' He comforts the thief dying alongside him who asks to be remembered by him in his kingdom, telling him, 'Truly I tell you, today you will be with me in Paradise.' And finally, he surrenders himself to his Father: 'Father, into your hands I commend my spirit' (Luke 23:34,43,46). Then in John's Gospel, he speaks three more words from the cross, words that indicate majesty, control. Jesus is in command of the situation. He commits his mother into the care of the beloved disciple, saying to his mother, 'Woman, here is your son,' and to his friend, 'Here is your mother.' He fulfils the Scriptures by asking for a drink: 'I am thirsty.' And, after drinking, he announces, 'It is finished,' then he bows his head and gives up his spirit (John 19:26, 27, 28, 30). There is, therefore, a pattern that develops in these narratives from desolation through compassion to control. And we should not forget that for John, Jesus being lifted up on the cross is to be understood as well as his being lifted up to resurrection, to triumph over death. John's is a unified vision.

It is always John's account that is read out when the Lord's Passion is commemorated on Good Friday, but I don't think, therefore, that Denis was wrong to self-isolate and mourn. The Johannine narrative may bring before us the majesty of the cross with Jesus in command, but the sacrifice of Jesus, our commemoration of his suffering and death, leads us also to a place of darkness and desolation. Good Friday can affect us in many ways. It is important that we do not allow ourselves to be distracted by the Easter glory that is about to shine forth.

People often react to the crucifixion in two contrasting ways. There are some who comment that Jesus' sufferings cannot have been so terrible because, being God, he knew it would soon be over and that he would rise again. But we should not suppose that the Lord was hanging there, comforted by secret knowledge. Then there are others who say that there is nothing they could suffer that could bear comparison with the sufferings of Jesus. But there is no reason to imagine that we cannot identify our sufferings with his.

We should contemplate seriously what he had to endure. His sufferings are not so different from ours.

There were physical sufferings: rough arrest, buffeting, mockery and humiliation, scourging, a crowning with thorns, nails driven through wrists and ankles, and the excruciating agony of crucifixion, levering himself up to escape asphyxiation which was the normal cause of death of those who were crucified. Eventually exhausted, they could no longer move and so could no longer breathe. They suffocated and died.

Then there were the personal sufferings, Judas's betrayal, Peter's denial, and the desertion of the others. For many years, however, I have thought that perhaps the most poignant, personal moment for Jesus was when he caught sight of his mother in the crowd as he was being led along the way to Calvary. If there had been one thought that may have comforted him in his Passion, it may perhaps have been his sense that he was fulfilling the Father's will. He may not have had, does not need to have had, a clear understanding of the implications of his mission or the way it was ending, but to know that he was in fact being faithful to the Father and that what he was doing brought completion, may have strengthened him. Everything was coming to a head, to fulfilment, in his Passion and death. And then he sees his mother in the crowd and realises that it is not so simple and that his sufferings, this completion, was not perfectly complete after all, because his sufferings were themselves the cause of suffering for her. The poignancy of that moment strikes me still, although it has been tempered more recently.

Some years ago Archbishop John Ha, who has now retired but was then the Archbishop of Kuching in Malaysia, invited me to Sarawak to direct a retreat for priests from his diocese and from the neighbouring diocese of Sibu. Before the retreat began, two priests whom I knew already, took me to the pastoral centre up the mountain at Singai. This centre had initially seemed destined to be a failure, but has since become a notable success. As we climbed the mountain to the centre, we prayed the Fourteen Stations of the Cross that punctuate the steep climb. These Stations recall moments in Jesus' Passion from his condemnation by Pilate to his burial, and one of those moments, the Fourth Station, is when Jesus sees his mother in the crowd. On this occasion, however, what struck me was not so much the poignancy of the meeting between mother and son; she must indeed have been grief-stricken at the sight of him, beaten, bruised, and bloodied, but that was not all. In the midst of the crowd, baying and mocking and delighting in his sufferings, it suddenly occurred to me that Jesus must also have been comforted because her eyes uniquely, in spite of sorrow, looked at him with unconditional love. Nevertheless, he was causing her sorrow too.

So Jesus suffered physically and personally, but there was spiritual suffering as well, expressed in that cry from the cross, 'My God, my God, why have you forsaken me?' The dark nights of the senses and of the spirit are not an experience from which Jesus was shielded. He too felt abandoned. As I have mentioned already, Mother Teresa experienced darkness. On one occasion she speaks insistently, in spite of the darkness, of her longing for God: 'To be in love and yet not to love, to live by faith and yet not to believe. To spend myself and yet to be in total darkness.'[2]. As I have said, there were those who, on learning of her experience of darkness, thought her a hypocrite, deceiving people, just pretending to be a woman of faith. They did not understand. They could not conceive such darkness. But Jesus embraced the darkness that he encountered in his Passion.

When we speak of the Passion of Jesus, we need to probe more deeply. We mean, of course, not only his death on the cross, but also his torture, the scourging and crowning with thorns, the suffering he endured that was brutal and extreme.

2 Quoted in Murray, *I Loved Jesus in the Night,* p.31.

And to understand it better it may help to notice something else. 'Passion' gives us the word 'passive'. Until his arrest, Jesus has been active, calling disciples, travelling the countryside, teaching and healing, casting out devils and working wonders. He has consistently been full of energy, taking the initiative. But, once under arrest, he becomes passive.[3] It is no longer a question of what he does, but of what is done to him. He has been handed over. He is mocked and beaten, interrogated and scourged, taken to Herod and returned to Pilate, tried and condemned, led out, nailed to the cross and crucified. The one who was always active is now helpless. He is passive. In the words of the prophet Isaiah, captured startlingly in Zubarán's painting, 'He was oppressed, and he was afflicted, yet he did not open his mouth; like a lamb that is led to the slaughter, and like a sheep that before its shearers is silent, so he did not open his mouth' (Isaiah 53:7).

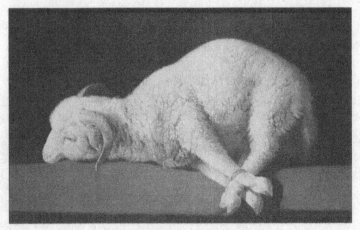

Francisco de Zubarán, *Agnus Dei*

3 See W. H. Vanstone, *The Stature of Waiting*, (London, Darton, Longman & Todd, 1982).

Being passive may suggest someone who is weak, but, although he is vulnerable, nothing in the Gospels has indicated weakness in Jesus. In his Passion he is indeed passive. But we need to remember that 'passion' gives us another word as well, it gives us 'passionate'.

Passionate people are not normally passive. On the contrary, they are charged with energy, but what drives them is something other than themselves. At its worst, they may be unhinged or out of control. They may be obsessed or self-absorbed, consumed by anger or hatred. Then their obsession, their self-absorption, their anger or hatred may control them. But it need not be so. At its best, passion can overwhelm us, but we do not lose control. Instead, it sets us free. It helps us to be true to ourselves.

Jesus in his Passion was passive. Outwardly he was indeed a victim, at the mercy of those who had arrested him. But within he was passionate. His Passion, the cause that overwhelmed him and drove him on, was his desire to be faithful in love.

Jesus was faithful. He was faithful in his love for the Father and faithful in his love for us. His faithful love for the Father meant that he was perfectly obedient to the Father's will. His faithful love for us meant that he was at the service of our deepest need. What was the Father's will? That we, men and women, estranged from him by our resistance to love which is the source of all evil and which we call sin, should cast that resistance aside and be reconciled to him. And what is our deepest need? To be reconciled. There was, therefore, a perfect correlation between the Father's will and our need. And Jesus was passionate about it.

Overwhelmed by his desire to effect that reconciliation, his own love knew no bounds. He accepted its consequences, whatever they might be – even death on the cross. Passionate, he became the passive victim, so that we might recognise in his sacrifice evidence of the Father's limitless love for us and be stirred to respond. And so be reconciled. Once reconciled, we in our turn are invited to share his Passion, to be as passionate as he was, as possessed by love as he was.

★

Holy Saturday

And so we come to Holy Saturday, the final day of the Triduum. The day before, Christians have commemorated Jesus' death on the cross; the day after, they will celebrate his resurrection; but on this day, this Sabbath between sunset on the Friday and sunset today, the Saturday, they remember that Jesus lies dead in his tomb. On this day, Christians and non-believers alike have, so to speak, a feast in common. They are in agreement. Jesus is dead and buried. In death he is inaccessible. We are abandoned. It is a time of desolation not to be tamed.

For those who take delight in the demise of Christianity, I suppose that every day is Holy Saturday, with Jesus dead and buried and gone for ever. But they need to be wary. Non-belief, as they will know, provides no safe haven from desolation or disaster. When they feel abandoned, where will they turn? Coherent secularism is like the golden calf in the wilderness. Those who invoke it in times of crisis will find it has eyes that cannot see and ears that cannot hear and lips that cannot speak. We are in the realm of faith. It may be that non-belief is truer than belief. Perhaps Christianity is false. But maybe not.

What we value is revealed in times of crisis. Then we are forced to take stock. Francesca Luard, gifted and beautiful, when she found she was dying from an AIDS-related illness, wrote, 'The only time I get religious is when I'm very unhappy. I place myself in God's hands as if I were a baby and I feel safe.'[4] Is that cowardice? I don't think so. In countries that are

4 See Elisabeth Luard, *Family Life: Birth, Death and the Whole Damn Thing*, (London, Corgi Books, 1996), p.274.

poorer economically than Great Britain, religious faith often flourishes. Is that no more than superstition or a strategy to cope with misfortune? We must take care not to patronise or condescend. Perhaps wisdom is breaking through. Both Christians and non-believers have something to learn from this day.

Holy Saturday is associated with Christ's descent into hell. Long ago scholars would debate how Jesus, if he were the saviour of all, could be the saviour of those who had died before he was born. Had an accident of time put them beyond his reach? And they found in this day, when the body of Jesus lay in the tomb, a way to resolve the conundrum. They taught that it commemorated Jesus entering the underworld, harrowing hell, and calling forth the just. In his own abandonment Jesus reached out to those who seemed to be beyond reach and restored them. Whatever might be thought about the origin of that idea, it reveals an instinct for profound truth, expressed with stunning power by George Mackay Brown in his poem which indeed he called *The Harrowing of Hell*.

He went down the first step.
His lantern shone like the morning star.
Down and round he went
Clothed in his five wounds.

Solomon whose coat was like daffodils
Came out of the shadows.
He kissed wisdom there, on the second step.

The boy whose mouth had been filled with harp-songs,
The shepherd king
Gave, on the third step, his purest cry.
At the root of the Tree of Man, an urn
With dust of apple-blossom.

Joseph, harvest-dreamer, counsellor of pharaohs,
Stood on the fourth step.
He blessed the lingering Bread of Life.

He who had wrestled with an angel,
The third of the chosen,
Hailed the King of Angels on the fifth step.

Abel with his flute and fleeces
Who bore the first wound
Came to the sixth step with his pastorals.

On the seventh step down
The tall primal dust
Turned with a cry from digging and delving.

Tomorrow the Son of Man will walk in a garden
Through drifts of apple-blossom.[5]

Christ harrows hell. Descending, he encounters Solomon, David, Joseph, Jacob, Abel and Adam, the tall primal dust. And then he walks in a garden through drifts of apple blossom. No horror lies beyond the healing power of the Son of Man. He has explored the very depths. For those who rejoice in Christianity, this message is an inspiration, for it means there is no sin that cannot be forgiven, or defeat that cannot become triumph, or sorrow that cannot be turned into joy. And for those who despise the gospel or regard it with indifference or find, perhaps with regret, that they simply cannot believe, it is a reminder: this message is for them as well; this day belongs to them as much as to Christians. They are under no duress. But should a crisis occur, or when the time comes to take stock, no

5 Archie Bevan and Brian Murray (eds.), *The Collected Poems of George Mackay Brown*, (London, John Murray, 2006), pp.400–1.

past contempt or indifference or unbelief is irreparable. There is no condition so extreme as to be beyond the reach of Jesus, abandoned and laid in the tomb. Out of the depths he calls us back to life.

9

Easter glory: Christ is risen

'Christ is risen!' That is the traditional cry of Easter night. What should not be missed, however, as the vigil celebration moves into the Mass of the Resurrection, is that there is no appearance of the risen Lord. His resurrection is proclaimed, but he is never seen. There may seem to be one exception to that. When the account is taken from the Gospel of Matthew, the women who have come to the tomb and found it empty, as they run away, are said to meet Jesus. We are told that they fall at his feet and worship him, but he instructs them, 'Do not be afraid; go and tell my brothers to go to Galilee; there they will see me.' These words are little more than an echo of what the angel whom they have met in the tomb has told them: 'Go quickly and tell his disciples, "He has been raised from the dead," and indeed he is going ahead of you to Galilee; there you will see him' (Matthew 28:10,7). The encounter with Jesus seems more like an editorial gloss. Whatever may be the case, when the resurrection is proclaimed, it comes as a summons to faith, not as a conclusion based on empirical experience. And the same is true on Easter Day itself. Peter and the beloved disciple run to the tomb, find it empty, and believe (John 20:3-8). But still they have not seen Jesus. And, while they believed, they may also have been bemused. What had happened?

Every Easter, theories are rehearsed in answer to that question. Did the disciples find the tomb empty because they had gone to the wrong one? Was the body of Jesus removed by persons unknown? Had it been stolen? Or perhaps Jesus survived his intended execution and was able to creep away. Such questions were reviewed afresh by Professor Geza Vermes in 2008 in his book, *The Resurrection*. His treatment was notable as always for the skill, sympathy and respect that he brought to the issues. He set these questions and theories in perspective and concluded by calling attention instead to the 'powerful mystical experience' that the first followers of Jesus underwent, something which changed their earlier cowardice into courage and impelled them to proclaim in public the good news that Jesus had preached and made known to them. The resurrection of Jesus refers, he argued, to his spiritual presence as a living reality in the hearts of those who feel he is close to them.[1]

The conclusion is moving, but still not quite satisfactory. All these explanations are straightforward: from a tomb identified as empty by mistake or theft, to an unexpected survival or a spiritual resurrection. A cynic might dismiss these descriptions as little more than an elevated version of the conviction that 'Elvis lives'. They are straightforwardly intelligible. They make no demands on faith. There is no extra dimension. But what was it that triggered that powerful mystical experience that transformed Jesus' first followers?

The accounts in the various Gospels of the risen Jesus are very different. The witnesses vary and the places where their encounters occurred with Jesus vary as well, conditioned by different theological approaches. In Matthew the disciples are told to go to Galilee, in John after seeing him first in Jerusalem they meet him once more by the Sea of Tiberias, while in Luke all the appearances of the risen Jesus take place in Jerusalem. These differences are significant because they put into relief what all these accounts have in common. Whatever the particular Gospel tradition, two elements recur.

1   Geza Vermes, *The Resurrection*, (London, Penguin Books, 2008), p.150.

There is always something immediate and physical. The women who run from the tomb in Matthew, and Mary Magdalene in John cling to the risen Christ; in John, Thomas is invited to place his finger into Jesus' wounded hands and his hand into his side; on other occasions, whether in the upper room in Jerusalem, at Emmaus, or by the lakeside, Jesus is said to eat with the disciples or he invites them to eat. At the same time, besides this physical immediacy there is also always something mysterious. Mary Magdalene, first of all, supposes Jesus to be the gardener; then, when he shows himself to the disciples in the upper room, we are told that he entered even though the door was locked; and the two disciples on the road to Emmaus fail to recognise him until he breaks bread with them at supper. There is also that more general expression in Matthew's Gospel when Jesus meets the disciples on the mountain in Galilee and we are told that, while some believed in him, nevertheless 'some doubted'.

This combination of the immediate and the mysterious is consistent. My favourite example is the scene by the Sea of Tiberias in John's Gospel when, after an unsuccessful fishing expedition, a figure on the shore calls to Peter and the others, encouraging them to cast their nets again. They do so and haul in an immense catch. They realise that the figure is Jesus. When they come ashore, they have breakfast with him. But we are told, 'Now none of the disciples dared to ask him, "Who are you?" because they knew it was the Lord' (John 21:12). If they knew him, why is 'daring' even mentioned?

As usual, these passages are not precise descriptions of events; instead they convey an experience. What is immediate expresses the realisation that the man who is with them is really there, physically present, recognisably the man they had known and loved and followed; what is mysterious indicates that he is not present as he had been before. This combination of the immediate and the mysterious reveals the unique quality of the disciples' privileged experience, offering us some insight into what overwhelmed and transformed them, something real, not of their making, an experience that transformed their cowardice into courage.

★

Among the disciples who had gone on that fishing expedition with Peter was Thomas. His first encounter with the risen Jesus is, of course, famous and has earned him the sobriquet, Doubting Thomas. The occasion is recounted in John's Gospel.

On the evening of the day when Mary Magdalene began to spread the word that she had met the crucified Jesus, risen from the dead, Jesus appeared to some of his disciples in the upper room. Although the doors were locked, he came among them and showed them the wounds in his hands and side. Here too, as we have noted, there was the mysterious element, locked doors, and the immediacy of the wounds. Thomas, however, was not with them. When the others told him what had happened, he was not convinced. 'Unless I see the mark of the nails in his hands,' he told them, 'and put my finger in the mark of the nails and my hand in his side, I will not believe' (John 20:25). And so the scene was set for that dramatic moment when doubting Thomas met the risen Jesus.

Eight days later, Jesus appeared in the upper room again. This time Thomas was there. And Jesus invited him to do what he had insisted he would have to do, if he were to believe, to put his finger in the wounded hands and his hand into the gash in Jesus' side. Artists like Caravaggio, seeking to capture the moment, have often shown Thomas doing so, but the text indicates it was not necessary. Thomas declared simply, 'My Lord and my God.' But then Jesus challenges him, 'Have you believed because you have seen me?' How often we say, 'Seeing is believing.' But is it? If Thomas believes only because he sees, we may wonder whether he really believes at all. As he sees, he has no need to believe. And indeed Jesus adds words that, as we have realised, have comforted many like the blind John Hull: 'Blessed are those who have not seen and yet have come to believe' (John 20:24–29). Isn't that the essence of faith, belief without sight?

Caravaggio, *The Incredulity of St Thomas*

Faith and doubt we normally regard as incompatible. But are they? Maybe not. Perhaps by doubting, Thomas has a lesson to teach us.

First, it is important to remember that Jesus' presence in that room was not like the presence of anyone else who was there. His resurrection was not resuscitation. He had not simply returned to life like Lazarus or Jairus's daughter. Once again, the Gospels tell us what happened, but not as a simple verbal photograph. We are taught about events by realising their significance. Jesus was really there, indicated, as we have just observed, by the way he had shown the disciples his wounds and then by inviting Thomas to touch him: he was not a figment of their imagination or a shared hallucination. Yet he came among them in spite of the doors being locked. Risen to new life, his was a presence of a different kind. He was not seen by those who did not believe. As another Thomas, St Thomas Aquinas, was to teach centuries later, the risen Lord was seen '*fide oculata*', by the eye of faith, the perceptiveness that faith bestows.[2] So as Thomas the disciple saw, he cannot have stopped believing. How then are we to understand his doubting? Faith and doubt may not be as incompatible as we had supposed.

Perhaps Thomas was not there when Jesus first appeared to the others, not through indifference, but because he was broken-hearted with grief and struggling with guilt because of his cowardice when his friend was arrested and put to death. After all, according to John, when Jesus had decided to disregard the dangers of going up to Jerusalem, Thomas had been the one to declare, 'Let us also go, that we may die with him' (John 11:16). But he had not died. He had deserted him like the rest. And so his grief and guilt. Maybe what we call his doubt, his reluctance to believe news that must have seemed too good to be true, was a fruit of remorse and love.

And there is more, for faith is matured when we realise that what we believe may not be accurate, or the way we understand what we believe may be mistaken. We must not forget that 'Blessed are those who mourn' is the beatitude for the scholar. There is a passage in Graham Greene's novel, *Monsignor Quixote*, when the old priest dreams that angels had saved Jesus from the cross. Instead of agony and death and the empty tomb, Jesus had stepped down in triumph, honoured by Jews and Romans alike, while his mother smiled through her tears: 'There was no ambiguity, no room for doubt and no room for faith at all. The whole world knew with certainty that Christ was the Son of God.' The old man then wakes, feeling the chill

2 Thomas Aquinas, *Summa Theologiae* III, art.55, q.2, ad 1.

of despair and praying to be delivered from the 'Saharan desert' of faith without doubt.[3] As Greene once remarked about himself to his friend, the Spanish priest Leopoldo Duran, 'The trouble is I don't believe my unbelief.' We may say we believe in the conclusions we have reached, but faith is at work at a level more fundamental than belief.[4]

Doubt need not be the enemy of faith but its ally. What Thomas believed, that Jesus had died, prevented him from accepting the news his friends gave him, that Jesus had risen. He doubted. In past centuries the doubt of one of Jesus' disciples was seen as an embarrassment, yet Thomas's questioning and then his unrestrained profession of faith also caused him to be regarded as a model theologian. Faith is deepened when we wrestle with ambiguity. Then indeed they are blessed who without seeing have come to believe. Thomas doubted and then believed. Gregory the Great once observed, 'To us, Thomas's unbelief was more profitable than the belief of the other disciples, for the fact that he was led to faith by touching confirms, in us, a faith from which all doubt is thus removed.' That may give us comfort, but not entirely convince. Those like Thomas who move from doubt to faith may not have come completely to rest. They may oscillate, doubting then believing, doubting then believing. But Gregory continued, 'God permitted his disciple to doubt in this way, after the resurrection, but did not desert him in his doubt.'[5] Now that is

3 Graham Greene, *Monsignor Quixote*, (London, The Bodley Head, 1982), p.67.

4 Greene's remark is quoted on the frontispiece of Leopoldo Duran's memoir, *Graham Greene: Friend and Brother*, (London, HarperCollins, 1994). See also John Wilkins, 'A Foot in the Door', *The Tablet*, 23 May 2020, pp.10–11.

5 Gregory the Great, *Homily* 26:7. See Alexander Murray, *Doubting Thomas in Medieval Exegesis and Art*, Conferenze 22, Unione Internazionale degli Istituti di Archeologia Storia e Storia dell'Arte in Roma, (Roma, Biblioteca Apostolica Vaticana, 2006), p.49.

comforting. When clouds of doubt cast shadows over our faith, we should not lose heart. Neither does the Lord desert us. We are not abandoned. Yet living by faith, being a disciple, is a risky business.

*

Risks can be fascinating. They give the gambler his thrill. But risks do not fall into a single category. Many years ago it occurred to me that there is an instructive distinction between the risks we run because we have taken an initiative and those that we face because we have accepted an invitation.

When we take an initiative – for example, to move house or change job or emigrate – we should, if we are wise, assess the implications. We weigh up the advantages and disadvantages. We know we don't control the outcome. What will happen is not guaranteed. We recognise that some risk is unavoidable. Things may go wrong. But if we decide to proceed, the risks we face can be described as of our own choosing. They are our risks. On the other hand, when we respond to a sense of vocation that will change our lives, such as a decision perhaps to marry, or change, not just a job, but a career, like a banker becoming a doctor, or to explore the possibility of priesthood or the religious life, we know that these decisions too, if taken, will involve risks. We don't know precisely how they will turn out. Once again, we look ahead and weigh up whether or not to accept. We think it through as best we can. And if we accept, we must take responsibility for the decision. But I would suggest that if we accept, the risks involved are different from those which are part of an initiative of our own that we may have taken. These risks that come from responding to a sense of vocation, are more like the acceptance of an invitation and, as such, are not of our own choosing. To accept such an invitation involves making a commitment. It means that we accept the risks, the consequences of that commitment, whatever they may be. We are following in the footsteps of the master who faithfully accepted the consequences of loving, whatever they might be, even to accepting death on a cross. Discipleship, the journey into light, is a risky business.

When Jesus called the fishermen, Simon and Andrew, James and John, they left everything – boats, nets, livelihood and family – to follow him (Mark 1:16–20). It was not as though they had noticed this man from Nazareth and weighed the consequences of following him. They were not like canny entrepreneurs, calculating a risk that might make their future more profitable. They had no idea what the outcome might be. They had not taken the initiative. Jesus had. As a friend of mine has often observed, 'Jesus didn't work with volunteers.' He called people, invited them to come with him. Not everyone did. Think of the rich young man who wanted to be perfect, but when he was told to go and sell everything he had, then to come and follow Jesus, the pull of his wealth was too strong. It is an incident to which we shall return. But while the young man turned away, the disciples did not. They took the risk of answering the call, without knowing where it would lead. They were far from perfect, as we have seen. They often missed the point, failed to understand what they were being taught, and, when crisis finally struck in Jerusalem, they were terrified and ran away. But they didn't scatter. They gathered in the upper room and Jesus came to them. They may have deserted him. He did not desert them.

*

The time that followed was a curious time. How long did it last before Jesus was taken from them, ascending into heaven? Luke in the Acts of the Apostles speaks of forty days: 'After his suffering he presented himself alive to them by many convincing proofs, appearing to them during forty days and speaking about the kingdom of God' (Acts 1:3). And yet in his Gospel Luke tells a different story. On the morning after the Sabbath Mary Magdalene and some other women go to the tomb, find it empty and immediately go and tell the apostles. 'That same day' two other disciples, we learn, are on the road to Emmaus and meet Jesus without recognising him until, during their supper together he breaks bread, but then disappears from their sight. 'That same hour' they return to Jerusalem and tell the eleven in the upper room what had happened to them. 'While they were talking', Jesus comes among them, shows them his wounds and asks for something to eat. He then explains the Scriptures to them: 'Thus it is written that the Messiah is to suffer and to rise from the dead on the third day, and that repentance and forgiveness of sins is to be proclaimed in his name to all nations, beginning from Jerusalem.' Afterwards he leads them out to Bethany, blesses them, and is 'carried up into heaven' (Luke 24:51). And it is still the evening of Easter day. So did the ascension take place that same day or was it after forty days, as recorded in Acts?

Numbers are important in the Scriptures. It is no coincidence that the people of Israel wandered in the wilderness for forty years, that Moses went up Mount Sinai for forty days and forty nights, that Elijah journeyed for forty days and forty nights to Mount Horeb, that Jesus went into the wilderness for forty days, after which, as we have reflected, he was tempted, or now that a period of forty days is mentioned between the Lord's resurrection and his ascension. We are not concerned with a particular measurement of time, but a privileged period of time. How long it was in fact we cannot tell.

A unifying theme of Luke's writing is the road to and from Jerusalem. Towards the end of the ninth chapter, we are told that Jesus set his face to go to Jerusalem (Luke 9:51). Thereafter the narrative contains regular, passing references to this journey on the way to Jerusalem. And, as we have just noticed – and predictably in Luke – the risen Jesus appears to the eleven only in Jerusalem and instructs them to proclaim the good news 'beginning from Jerusalem'. And in the Acts of the Apostles, Luke tells the story of that mission, beginning from

Jerusalem and spreading abroad, ending in Rome. That the ascension took place on that first day, as narrated in the Gospel, suits Luke's theological vision of the road that leads to Jerusalem and then in Acts leads away from it in every direction to the ends of the earth. But the forty days mentioned in the book of Acts seems, in fact, more likely to represent what happened, not as a precise period, but as a privileged period during which the disciples encountered Jesus, a period that ended before Pentecost which is celebrated fifty days after the feast of Passover.

We may wonder why these meetings between Jesus and his disciples ceased. Once risen from the dead to new life, why did they not just go on and on? Why should they stop? When I wonder about that question, I think about Bernadette Soubirous in Lourdes. On 11 February 1858, this fourteen-year-old, illiterate peasant girl, while collecting firewood by the river Gave, saw a lady whom she called in the local dialect, *Aquerò*, That Thing, and she came to recognise that she was having a vison of the Mother of Jesus. She saw her on a further seventeen occasions, until 16 July that same year, and never again. The visions occurred during a particular and limited period of time. I am not suggesting that Bernadette's visions of Mary were comparable to the experiences of Jesus' disciples between the resurrection and ascension, but they may help us appreciate that profound spiritual experiences can take place within a limited period of time. They don't need to go on indefinitely. They may also serve a purpose. They may indicate a time of transition. Perhaps that is what this privileged period was for the disciples: a time of transition between the Passion of Jesus and the outpouring of the Spirit at Pentecost.

*

The Easter season ends with the feast of Pentecost, the day described in the Acts of the Apostles when the Holy Spirit came down on those who were gathered in the upper room.

There was the sound like a rushing, violent wind, and flames like fire are said to have appeared among them, and, when the apostles spoke, we are told that the different people who were living in Jerusalem at that time heard them speaking, each in his own native language (Acts 2:1–6). In the 1960s, when I was a student in Rome, I was lucky enough to hear the Canadian Jesuit, David Stanley, reflecting on this event. One point has made a lasting impression on me.

I remember Stanley remarking in relation to Pentecost that there was no nostalgia in the New Testament. He referred to the way people nowadays will sometimes say how much they wish they could have seen Jesus during his public ministry. They explain that it would strengthen their faith and help them to pray, if they knew what Jesus had looked like, if they had heard the sound of his voice, if they had seen how he walked. They look back to the public ministry of the Christ as to a golden age. How unlucky we are to have missed it.

At first, this reaction may seem natural enough, but, Stanley observed, it is a view which is utterly foreign to the New Testament. There is no trace of it there. Nobody is looking back nostalgically. Thomas, it is true, as we have noticed, wanted to be able to put his finger into the wounded hands and his hand into Jesus' side, but that was not nostalgia. He wanted proof to conquer his doubt, to overcome his grief. So why was there no nostalgia? It is because, Stanley answered, for the writers of the New Testament the public ministry of Jesus was not the golden age – for them that began with this outpouring of the Holy Spirit. That was the start of the golden age. It runs from Pentecost to the second coming of Jesus. Why look back? This is the golden age. We are living in it now.

That idea may very well take us by surprise, but perhaps the idea of a golden age needs to be defined more precisely. It may appear superficially to suggest a perfect time when all our problems are solved and our desires are satisfied. And our present age is not like that. We live under the real threat of the pandemic, and elsewhere there is war, violence and tyranny, poverty, human trafficking and the misery inflicted on refugees. An Age, however, is not defined only by events. It is defined more significantly by its spirit. But there is more than one spirit abroad and a crucial question asks, which spirit is guiding us? Which spirit are we welcoming? Is it the spirit of greed or of generosity? Is it a selfish spirit or the Spirit of love? Is it the spirit of death or the Spirit of life?

Pentecost should make us reflect on the Spirit of the golden age, a Spirit of forgiveness and reconciliation, inspired by love. A friend once quoted to me a saying of St Francis de Sales: 'There is good in everyone. The fun lies in finding it.' It certainly captures his spirit. And the Holy Spirit has been called the delight of God. That is the Spirit poured out at Pentecost and offered to us still. In these demanding days, if we will receive this Spirit, we can overcome the challenges that confront us.

IO

Pentecostal breath and fire: the birth of the Church

Pentecost, when the Holy Spirit descended on the apostles, is often referred to as the birthday of the Church. The apostles received the promise of the Spirit in Luke's Gospel before Jesus ascended into heaven with the words: 'I am sending upon you what my Father promised' (Luke 24:49), and similarly in Acts when Jesus ordered them not to leave Jerusalem, but to wait there for the promise of the Father (Acts 1:4–5). And their experience, when this promise was fulfilled, was associated with wind and fire, 'a sound like the rush of a violent wind' and 'divided tongues, as of fire' (Acts 2:2–3). Notice what is being said. A careful reading reveals something quite subtle. Those gathered in the upper room did not find themselves suddenly having to survive a hurricane; the sound that filled the house was '*like* the rush of a violent wind'. Nor were they in danger of incineration; what appeared to rest on them were tongues '*as of* fire' (Acts 2:2–3). So, not actually wind and fire, but wind and fire are the strong, vivid, living images that Luke used to express this outpouring of the Spirit on these followers of Jesus, bringing the Church to birth.

Luke's account of Pentecost, however, is not the only story of the Church's birth. In John's Gospel, it was at the Last Supper that Jesus promised his disciples that they would receive the Holy Spirit. He told them, 'The Advocate, the Holy Spirit, whom the Father will send in my name, will teach you everything, and remind you of all that I have said to you' (John 14:26). The

Advocate or the Paraclete is counsel for the defence. And it is noteworthy that he will help the disciples to remember all they had learnt from Jesus. He is the agent of remembrance. And, in this Gospel, Jesus fulfils his promise on Easter night. When he appeared in the upper room, we are told that he breathed on the disciples and said to them, 'Receive the Holy Spirit' (John 20:22). If the outpouring of the Spirit that is promised in Luke's Gospel (Luke 24:49) and Acts (Acts 1:4–5) is fulfilled at Pentecost, in the Johannine writings, what is promised at the Last Supper is fulfilled on Easter evening. According to John, as Jesus being lifted up on the cross can be understood as his being lifted up both to die and to rise from death – a unified vision of the paschal mystery – so it is in tune with that unified vision for the disciples to receive the Spirit on Easter night.

I find something especially intriguing about John's idea of the Spirit that reminds the disciples of all they have learnt from Jesus. Memory is fascinating. Over the years, I realise that I have listened to innumerable lectures, homilies and sermons, and sometimes I've asked myself with a wry inward smile how much of what I have heard I could remember. There has not been much. Some things have stuck, like those lectures given by David Stanley in Rome, but those occasions have been rare. Then I think how, for more than fifty years, I have myself spoken in public virtually every day, lecturing or giving talks, and preaching at Mass, sometimes briefly, sometimes at greater length, sometimes more than once on the same day. And I smile again ironically, wondering how much anyone remembers of what I have said. Not much, I would guess. And I wonder where that material has come from; of course, from experience and reading, and from study and reflection, but I am aware as well of a reservoir of knowledge that has assisted what I have been saying, even though I am not conscious of everything the reservoir contains. How often do we find ourselves remembering things we haven't thought of for years? And I certainly cannot always remember the source, but ideas, thoughts, images have accumulated. Perhaps it is the Spirit who nourishes the memory.

I am drawn to thinking that our openness to the presence of the Spirit, the welcome we give to the Spirit, is what brings to mind that we have been taught. Writing to the Corinthians, Paul tells them, 'No one can say "Jesus is Lord" except by the Holy Spirit' (1 Corinthians 12:3). Anyone, of course, can utter those words physically, 'Jesus is Lord, Jesus is Lord', but that cannot be the point Paul is making. He is indicating that no one can utter those words and invest them with the significance they possess except by the Spirit. It is the presence of the Spirit that reminds us and transforms a simple sentence into a profession of faith. Furthermore, the Spirit is present as gift. Through that presence we can let God be God in our lives, so that the depth, the power and the glory of faith can flower. If we are open, the Spirit breathes in us and brings to mind what we have been taught. And what we have been taught has come to us, not from our own resources, but as gift.

★

In the weeks immediately following Pentecost, as we return to Ordinary Time, three major feasts are celebrated.

The Feast of the Most Holy Trinity

The first Sunday after Pentecost is always Trinity Sunday. It seems bizarre to have a feast of God alongside feasts of saints, even those who are best known, like Benedict, Francis and Dominic, Teresa of Avila and Bernadette, and yet it may be no bad thing to set aside a day quite deliberately each year to contemplate the divine mystery, to contemplate God, and especially to reflect on our vocation to share divine life.

It took centuries for the Church to articulate its faith in God as Three and God as One, although the New Testament, in speaking of God, speaks plainly of God as Father and Son and Spirit. To give familiar examples, the apostles are to baptise people 'in the name of the Father and of the Son and of the Holy Spirit' (Matthew 28:19), and Paul blesses the Corinthians, exclaiming, 'The grace of the Lord Jesus Christ, the love of God, and the communion of the Holy Spirit be with all of you' (2 Corinthians 13:13). But I don't want simply to repeat here what I have tried to explain elsewhere.[1] I would rather explore, when contemplating the Trinity, what it means for us to share in divine life and how that might be possible. The Johannine account of the Church's birth supplies us with a helpful starting point. John refers to the Spirit as the one who reminds us of all that Jesus has taught us, creating, as I have suggested, a reservoir of knowledge, a reservoir of which we may not always be fully conscious, a reservoir that is gift.

At the Last Supper, a fascinating statement is placed on Jesus' lips. Jesus describes the Spirit to the disciples as the Spirit of truth, sent by the Father in his name. As such, he says, the Spirit will guide them into all that is true. He will lead them to the complete truth. He will do so because he is not simply speaking from himself. What the Spirit teaches them will be taken from what belongs to Jesus. He will teach them everything, reminding them, as we have noticed already, of all that they have learnt from Jesus, all that belongs to Jesus (John 14:26). But it doesn't end there. A little later, he continues, 'All that the Father has is mine. For this reason I said that he (the Spirit) will take what is mine and declare it to you' (John 16:13–15). So what belongs to Jesus is not his exclusively, but is what he has received from the Father: 'All that the Father has is mine.' *Everything* the Father has belongs also to Jesus, the Son, not just a part of it. What the Spirit teaches comes from Jesus and what Jesus has been teaching comes from the Father. Father, Son and Spirit are perfectly one.

1 Strange, *The Catholic Faith*, pp. 177–86.

Andrei Rublev, *Icon of the Most Holy Trinity*

The Father is the Creator and his Word, the Son, is his perfect self-expression. The Word is not a perfect self-expression in the way that a writer might write a brilliantly exact and honest autobiography or a painter might paint a self-portrait that is considered a masterpiece. The perfection of the Word, the Son, as the perfect self-expression of the Father is of a different order. The Word is not merely an utterance. Father and Word are so perfectly united that they are indeed one. But they can be seen as distinct in so far as there is this relationship between them, so that the Father is not the Son, and the Son is not the Father. It was the Son, the Word who became flesh, the Son who was born, lived among us and was crucified and died, and was raised from the dead, not the Father.

The Spirit has often been described as the love that binds Father and Son in union. But in the Godhead that love is not merely a disposition. As the Son, the Word, is not just an utterance, but the perfect self-expression of the Father, and as such one with the Father, except for their relationship, so the Spirit is not just a disposition, but indeed the perfect loving bond that unites Father and Son and as such is one with them, united to them, and distinct too only because of his relationship with them. As Spirit, the Spirit is neither Father nor Son, nor are they the Spirit. It was the Spirit who was breathed onto the disciples at Easter and erupted onto them at Pentecost, not the Father or the Son. Within the Godhead, because of their relationships, Father, Son and Spirit are three distinct persons in one God.

But how can we make sense of the claim that we share in this divine life? We need to remember, first, that the Son, the Word who became flesh, was perfectly human, as we are; and because he truly shares our human nature, because he is one of us, sharing everything we have, he reveals our capacity to share everything he has, and so his divine nature as well.

Analogies are always limited, but it may help to consider records. When someone accomplishes something remarkable for the first time, Edmund Hillary climbing Everest, Roger Bannister running a mile in less than four minutes, we applaud their achievement, but there is a sense in which we are also applauding ourselves. No one perhaps has expressed it more exactly than Neil Armstrong. When he first stepped onto the surface of the moon on 20 July 1969, it was not only, as he said, 'one small step for a man', it was also truly 'one giant leap for mankind'. His small step made all men and women moon walkers. At that moment he was the only person ever to have done it, but his step revealed that human beings were capable of walking on the moon. None of us will become further persons in the Godhead, but because Jesus, our brother, a human being, one of us, is also truly divine, truly a person in the Godhead, he reveals the height and the depth of human capacity for intimacy with God. Although by adoption, not by nature, we are all called to share in divine nature, and we are capable of realising that vocation. As Jesus went on to say, 'Those who love me will keep my word, and my Father will love them, and we will come to them and make our home with them' (John 14:23). By our remaining faithful in love, the Father and the Son make their home in us.

And what part does the Spirit play in making this indwelling and shared life a reality? We can return to one of those images for the Spirit, not the violent rushing wind, nor the fire, but breath.

In the upper room on Easter night, as we have noticed, Jesus breathed on the disciples. He breathed on them and said, 'Receive the Holy Spirit.' Where there is breath, there is life. What enlivens us? What enthuses us? We can tell what enthuses people because it comes regularly into their conversations. People in love, as the saying goes, are constantly 'naming the beloved'. I am not encouraging people to become pious bores who usually do more harm than good. But that openness to the Spirit that we noticed earlier can be transformative. It makes us alert to the Spirit's presence, for, as Paul memorably told the Corinthians, 'we have received not the spirit of the world, but the Spirit that is from God so that we can under-stand the gifts bestowed on us by God.' And then he contin-ued: 'And we speak of these things in words not taught by human wisdom but taught by the Spirit, interpreting spiritual things to those who are spiritual' (1 Corinthians 2:12–13). These few lines are telling us a great deal. They are saying first that we have received the Spirit from God, and they are also stating that we receive the Spirit for a purpose, namely to understand God's gifts to us. And moreover, what we have received, we are to pass on to others, empowered by the Spirit, interpreting the things of the Spirit to those who in their turn have the sensitivity to welcome them. We are to interpret spiritual things to those who are spiritual.

Elsewhere Paul also spoke of the Spirit bearing witness with our spirit, so that we are able to cry out to God as Abba, as Father, supporting us when we are weak. He felt able to reassure the Romans: 'The Spirit helps us in our weakness; for we do not know how to pray as we ought, but that very Spirit intercedes with sighs too deep for words. And God, who searches the heart, knows what is the mind of the Spirit, because the Spirit intercedes for the saints according to the will of God' (Romans 8:26–7). We should ponder and recognise the intimacy with God that these words imply.

To speak of the Spirit's presence, however, is not special pleading or a claim to superiority, but rather a matter of acknowledging that, as some people have an ear for music and some have an eye for art, so there are those who are sensitive to this presence and blessed with the gift of faith. I think of the many people over the years who have come to talk with me for weeks on end, exploring Catholic Christianity and wondering whether it is a way of life they can embrace. Many have done so. But I would also want to add that there have been others who have decided eventually that they cannot proceed further. They are glad to be better informed about Catholicism, but it is not something that in all honesty they can accept. I find these people impressive as well. A crucial lesson I learn from them is the importance for those who do believe to try to live their faith ever more authentically. We hold our faith in trust for others.

And that authentic faith, to be lived more deeply, needs to be nourished. Nourishment can take many forms in the life of faith, not least, as we noticed earlier, by prayer, penance and service. But it is also nourished very evidently in the sacraments.

*

The Feast of Corpus Christi

Catholic Christianity teaches that there are seven sacraments: three sacraments of initiation, baptism, confirmation and Eucharist; two of healing, reconciliation and the anointing of the sick; and two of communion, marriage and holy orders. But these sacraments are not just rites to be performed. They are rooted in the Christ. Christ is the primordial sacrament, the sacrament of our encounter with God.[2] It is through Jesus who is the Christ, our brother and redeemer, that we come to have access to a share in divine life. But it is his humanity that offers us that access. There is an issue here that needs to be faced: how can such access be available to us when in the body he is absent?

When Jesus was raised from the dead and ascended into glory, he had indeed departed from us. However, during what we have now come to recognise as the golden age, that is, between Pentecost and the *parousia*, his second coming at the end of time, we have to manage 'without encountering Christ in the body'. It is not enough to recall events that took place long ago in Palestine, nor to deepen our personal devotion to the Christ as 'living, glorified and invisibly active in our lives', important as those aspects may be. Something more is necessary. As Edward Schillebeeckx has observed: 'Christ makes his presence among us actively visible and tangible too, not directly through his own bodiliness, but by extending among us on earth in visible form the function of his bodily reality which is

2 Schillebeeckx, *Christ the Sacrament*, pp.40–45.

in heaven. This precisely is what the sacraments are: the earthly extension of the "body of the Lord."[3]

The 'Word made flesh' was not, therefore, a mere event in human history for about thirty-three years twenty centuries ago. To quote Schillebeeckx again, it is '*as man* that the Son is the mediator of grace; he is the mediator in his humanity. His human mediation of grace therefore presupposes his corporeality'. It follows that 'if Christ did not make his heavenly bodiliness visible in some way in our earthy sphere, his redemption would after all no longer be for us; redemption would no longer turn its face towards us. Then the human mediation of Christ would be meaningless. Once he had completed the work of redemption, there would no longer be any reason for the existence of Christ's humanity.'[4] But the humanity of Jesus has eternal significance. It is the sacraments that make the incarnate Christ, human as well as divine, present to us. Sacraments share in, and are part of, the reality they symbolise.

Christ is really present in every sacrament, but the reality of that presence is identified in a particular way with the Eucharist. The gift of the Eucharist is what we celebrate specifically on this feast of Corpus Christi. The Eucharist, as we have considered, was instituted at the Last Supper when Jesus took the bread and the cup and, to the bewilderment of his disciples, identified the bread as his body that would be broken for them and the wine as his blood that would be poured out for them. And they were themselves to do what he was now doing as a memorial of him. What sense could they make of that, until the following day when they saw his abused, tortured body on the cross and his blood draining from his many wounds, and when, soon afterwards, he appeared to them, raised from the dead? Before long, they

---

3 Schillebeeckx, *Christ the Sacrament*, p.41.
4 ibid., pp.42, 43.

came to recognise Christ as their own paschal lamb who had been sacrificed (1 Corinthians 5:7). And when he had been raised, he ate with his followers in the upper room and by the lakeside in Galilee, and, most notably when he had supper with those two disciples on the road to Emmaus who at first had failed to recognise him. Then he took bread, blessed and broke it, and gave it to them, and at that moment their eyes were opened, and he disappeared from their sight. At once they said to each other, 'Were not our hearts burning within us while he was talking to us on the road, while he was opening the scriptures to us?' (Luke 24:30–2) It was the taking, blessing, breaking and distributing of bread, those essential eucharistic actions, that triggered this recognition. What he had done, his disciples came to do in memory of him.

This memorial of his suffering, death and resurrection is celebrated at the Eucharist, but speaking of the reality of Christ's presence has prompted a particular difficulty. The Scriptures say that Christ suffered once for all. The Letter to the Hebrews declares that 'Christ had offered for all time a single sacrifice for sins' (Hebrews 10:12). To speak, therefore, of the reality of Christ's presence at the celebration of Mass has suggested to some people not a single offering, made once and for all, but endless repetition. When a Mass is celebrated, is the Christ being made to suffer all over again? He is not. It is good to be aware of three concepts: memory, time and word, and to recognise how they are related to one another.

All three can be understood in two different ways. Memory, remembering past events, can be passive. We recall events, whether happy or sad, that year by year recede further away from us. We think back to a first meeting with someone whom we came to love or the loss of a dear friend who has died. But memory can also be active. We remember an incident that proved to be a turning-point in our life, a memory that is always present to us and a source of inspiration. On my first visit to Israel, in 1989, a memorial to the Six-Day War in 1967 was pointed out to me; it struck me powerfully that this memorial was not a merely passive reminder of that conflict, but a way of recalling that struggle that made it present. Then time may usually be thought of quantitatively, minutes, hours, days, weeks, months, years and so on. But time is also qualitative. We have been considering Christmastide, Passiontide, Eastertide. We have been thinking of times in the year marked by a particular quality. And should a friend have sudden, unexpected good news, we laugh and sometimes say, 'He thought all his Christmases had come at once.' Here too, a particular kind of time. And while words may be static, naming objects, trees and flowers, houses and gardens, they can also be dynamic, for example, as declarations of love or words of blessing. When we bless, it expresses what we hope for a person; when God blesses, it is done: 'Let there be light, and there was light' (Genesis 1:3). The Mass as memorial is neither passive, a nostalgic gazing back to an event that took place long ago, nor is it preoccupied with a moment in time that is receding into the ever more distant past, but it is active, making that particular event present at this time, in the present moment, making it present now. And the words spoken, especially during the eucharistic prayer, are not static words, simply repeating the words that Scripture tells us the Lord spoke at the Last Supper, 'This is my body, this is my blood,' but they are dynamic words – words of blessing – that effect what they signify. The Mass is not a repetition of Christ's death on Calvary, but a gathering at the foot of the cross. We are present in that place, at that time, privileged to be present at the scene of our redemption. We are there. And we are gathered as the body of the Lord, as the Church. All this is celebrated on the feast of Corpus Christi.

*

Reflecting on the Trinity, God as three and God as one, we have considered more specifically how we are invited to share divine life. At Corpus Christi we have pondered on the way that life is nourished sacramentally by Christ as the primordial sacrament, whose humanity mediates to ours an abiding call to that life and who nourishes us as well through the Eucharist. The sacraments, as Schillebeeckx affirmed, are the earthly extension of the body of Christ. And he went on to add at once that the body of Christ 'is the Church'.[5]

In the aftermath of Pentecost, we contemplate the Church coming to birth, at first through the presence of the Spirit opening us to a share in the life of God and then through the presence of Christ, especially in the wonder of the Eucharist. And the third of these great feasts after Pentecost is the feast of the founders of the Church of Rome, Peter and Paul. But it is Peter, in particular, who captures our attention immediately, as the petrine office has been controversial.

*

The Feast of St Peter and St Paul

Peter's leadership of the Twelve is evident from the Gospels and the Acts of the Apostles. Although impetuous and at times rebuked by Jesus, Peter is nevertheless the one appointed to be the rock, supporting the faith on which the community was to be built (Matthew 16:18), and he was commanded to strengthen the faith of the others (Luke 22:32) and to feed the flock (John 21:15–19) – all responsibilities laid on him, as we can see, in the three principal Gospel traditions. And in the Acts of the Apostles Peter is seen to be fulfilling those responsibilities, although to say that is not to suppose that there was immediate clarity about the character of the office he had been commissioned to undertake. It took centuries for an understanding of the petrine ministry as such to emerge. At first, appealing to Peter's successor, the Bishop of Rome, to settle disputes was a

5 Schillebeeckx, *Christ the Sacrament*, p.41.

matter of practicality that had arisen as the Christian community expanded and grew across the known world. It took a long time for this ministry to be recognised not simply as of practical use, but as possessing profound theological roots. It came to be seen not just as an office personal to Peter, but one that would also be needed in every generation, to support the faith of the Church, and to strengthen and nourish it.[6]

What has often been contentious, especially since the nineteenth century, however, has been the papal claim to infallibility, a claim defined as a dogma of the Church at the First Vatican Council in 1870. It has often been assumed to mean that everything a pope says must be true. Anthony McCarten, for example, in his book, *The Two Popes*, a dual biography of Pope Benedict XVI and Pope Francis, focuses on what he sees as the dilemma of there being two popes, one retired and one in office. As both are infallible, who is to be believed if they disagree? How can they both be infallible? This question gives the book its edge, but it is entirely wrongheaded.

The dilemma on which the book hinges does not exist. Infallibility is not an internal, personal gift with which a person, once elected pope, is endowed, so that he is indisputably correct on all essential matters relating to the Church for as long as he is alive. It is an external gift, integral to the office that he exercises in his service of the Church. There are no circumstances, therefore, in which a pope, once retired, like Benedict, can be regarded as infallible. He is retired. He no longer exercises papal ministry. Furthermore, McCarten refers to transcripts of Francis's morning homilies in the chapel of Santa Marta being published, because, he remarks, 'they are considered to be divinely inspired'.[7] But they are not. This too

---

6 See Strange, *The Catholic Faith*, pp.68–80. For a history of the papacy, see Eamon Duffy, *Saints and Sinners: A History of the Popes*, (London, Yale University Press, 4th edition, 2014).

7 Anthony McCarten, *The Two Popes*, (London, Penguin Books, 2019), p.200.

is a mistake. Popes are not inspired. Inspiration is internal. But infallibility, to repeat, is an external gift and exercised only in very precise circumstances and according to particular conditions. What might those circumstances and conditions be?

Popes will, of course, often speak about matters concerning faith and morals – what the faithful are to believe and how they are to behave – but they do so infallibly only rarely, in the most solemn circumstances, and usually to clarify definitively an issue that has been in dispute. Such crucial matters relate to the very heart of the faith, that is to say, to what has been revealed. Moreover it is this teaching that clarifies and deepens our understanding of Christian identity, of what it means to be a follower of Jesus Christ. But even then, what is proclaimed solemnly does not exhaust everything that can be said about the matter. That is the reason why infallible statements are described as negative. In the future there may be more to be said, not contradicting what has been defined, but developing it.

This link between identity and self-knowledge is vital. To be ourselves truly and healthily we need to know ourselves at least sufficiently. This truth makes me remember an occasion in the 1980s when I walked into my office one morning in the Oxford University Catholic Chaplaincy and a man was standing there who pointed at me and declared, 'I am the Pope and you are under obedience to me.' Needless to say, this was not Pope John Paul II on a private, unannounced, personal visit to me, but a man I knew well and liked. His mental health was fragile and he had evidently stopped taking the medication he needed to keep him more balanced. As his mental health had dipped, his grasp on his identity had frayed. To be ourselves in a healthy way we need to know ourselves. We don't need to have perfect self-knowledge. It is to be hoped that we will go on growing in self-knowledge all our lives. But we need to have enough self-knowledge because, if we don't, like my visitor that morning, our grip on our identity becomes blurred.

And what is true for individuals is true also for groups of people, for communities, for the Church.

When serious disputes arise that threaten the Church's identity, within Catholicism it is the Pope who ultimately has the authority to resolve the matter. I believe it helps to see the papal ministry in those terms, not as an office that imposes further teachings on us, but as a service to the Church, discerning and interpreting the mind of the Church, articulating our self-knowledge, our self-understanding, so that we can live out our identity more genuinely, truthfully, and profoundly. As such, it is a ministry that brings the Church to birth and helps to guide us into the light.

11

Becoming kingdom

After Eastertide and after considering the major feasts that follow, we return directly once more to Ordinary Time, when we explore and contemplate faith and its implications. We pick up where we left off between the Christmas season and the beginning of Lent. And it may be helpful to begin by wondering again about prayer. Many years ago, a friend came to see me who wanted to talk about developing his spiritual life. He was evidently a person who took these matters seriously, so I began by asking him the natural question: 'How do you begin to pray?' He told me that he began each morning by saying the Our Father. Then, after a slight pause, he added memorably, 'It usually takes me about twenty minutes.' He wasn't boasting. He was just giving me information.

In Luke's Gospel we are told that once, when Jesus had been praying, one of his followers asked him to teach them how to pray and it was then that he taught them what we now call the Lord's Prayer, the Our Father (Luke 11:1-4). In Matthew's account, however, Jesus teaches it during the Sermon on the Mount (Matthew 6:9–13). We know it so well. Or do we?

Long ago in a school where I was chaplain, a colleague of mine, before he had become a teacher, had been part of a British meteorological expedition in Antarctica. One day, an aircraft had taken off on a flight to survey the area, but had then been caught in a sudden, severe change in the weather, typical of the region. Visibility became so poor that the crew was completely disorientated. Whether instruments had failed or whether the conditions had become so extreme that they were of little practical use, I don't know, but it became necessary to locate the flight and talk it back to land. Other national stations were alerted, doing all they could to help in the crisis. And in the midst of this chaotic situation the pilot was heard saying, 'Our Father . . . Our Father . . . Our Father who art in heaven . . . who art in heaven . . . what comes next?' And so my friend led the pilot, phrase by phrase, through the Lord's Prayer, a prayer that the man could no longer remember. Perhaps he hadn't said it in years. And he landed safely.

Should there be anyone reading this whose memory of the prayer is also weak, let me offer this reminder:

Our Father
who art in heaven,
hallowed be thy name.
Thy kingdom come,
thy will be done,
on earth as it is in heaven.
Give us this day our daily bread
and forgive us our trespasses,
as we forgive those who trespass against us,
and lead us not into temptation,
but deliver us from evil. Amen.

It may seem extraordinary at first that a prayer which has become so familiar to so many people, if not that pilot, should absorb someone like that friend of mine for so long every day. And yet the words invite us to return again and again, not for precise analysis, but to ponder. Everyone will find something different.

*

For me the hub of the prayer, its central petition, is 'Thy kingdom come'. That is the request and indeed the desire that seems to drive the prayer as a whole. And whose kingdom is it? It is the Father's kingdom. Which Father? The one who is in heaven and who is defined by holiness: 'hallowed be thy name'. This name is not arbitrary; it identifies who the Father is. It does so by calling him holy. Holiness is not a property, something the Father has; it is rather code for God's identity: the Father is holy.

Then we cast our central petition in fresh terms. The kingdom we pray for is that condition where this holy Father's will is realised perfectly. And so we pray that the kingdom may come among us through his will being perfectly fulfilled, not only in heaven, but here on earth as well: 'thy will be done on earth as it is in heaven.' May earth reflect heaven.

These aspirations, however, may seem all too vague. What can it mean in practice to fulfil God's will among us, in our world, our society and culture? Instead of an answer, we seem to change tack. For next we pray, 'Give us this day our daily bread.' But the shift is more apparent than real. The bread we seek is not a daily square meal, vital as that may be. Beyond ordinary food we are asking for something more profound: to be sustained in our service of the kingdom. We are praying, 'Give us what we need this day and every day to make the kingdom come on earth as it is in heaven, so that we may be its true servants.' Catholics, of course, and many other Christians as well, would see that sustenance, that daily bread, realised in an outstanding way in the Eucharist. That is the daily food which sustains many of us for service.

All the same, the question returns. What does it mean in fact to make the kingdom come among us, to fulfil the divine will day by day?

At the very core of gospel service is forgiveness. Refreshed by daily bread, whatever that may be for each of us, we ask for our sins to be forgiven: 'Forgive us our trespasses.' We want to be reconciled to the Father. And we want to extend that reconciliation to others, to establish a culture of reconciliation.

Linked to our plea for forgiveness, therefore, is the pledge we make to forgive others who may have injured us. Although we may have been victims, we too forgive 'those who trespass against us'.

And we end with two further petitions: 'Lead us not into temptation, but deliver us from evil.' They are connected. First, in our service of the kingdom, we ask not to be assailed from within, not to be put under pressure by our own restless, still imperfect hearts that may so easily give way and sin again, damaging the reconciliation we have received. When we pray not to be led into temptation, we are not imagining that God is testing us perversely. We are asking to be protected from our own perversity. Then besides the temptation that may strike from within, we ask also to be protected from the evil that is external to us; we beg to be delivered from that evil as well.

The Lord's Prayer which seeks to make the kingdom come on earth as it is in heaven, is asking the Father to heal us within so that we may bring healing to others. The kingdom that we desire to make real among us is not esoteric. It encourages us to forgive and work for reconciliation internationally and nationally, in our homes and in our hearts. The challenge is demanding. How are we to rise to it?

The question makes me think of Monsignor James Sullivan. Jim Sullivan was unforgettable. He was born in 1903 and died in January 1999. He was the last President of the English College in Lisbon that prepared people for ministerial priesthood. It was a post that he held from 1948 till 1973. After that, he lived at the English College in Rome from 1977 to 1997, which is where I occasionally met him. Frail health eventually forced him to return to England. He had been ordained in 1929, so he was a priest for almost seventy years. At his diamond jubilee, he had remarked, 'I spent the first thirty years of my priesthood trying to bring people into the kingdom. I've spent the last thirty years trying to bring the kingdom into people.' Our Father, thy kingdom come, on earth as in heaven. How do we bring the kingdom into people? In other words, how do we help them to become kingdom?

Jesus came to proclaim the kingdom. 'The kingdom,' he declared, 'is close at hand.' In the Beatitudes he said of those who are poor in spirit and those who are persecuted for right-eousness' sake, 'theirs *is* the kingdom of heaven' (Matthew 5:8,10), a present reality. And there is also a sequence of seven parables in Matthew's Gospel that offers images of the king-dom (Matthew 13). And if the notion of the kingdom seems alien to some people today, even those who are citizens of the United Kingdom, it is noteworthy that the teaching in these parables depends largely on rural images, sowing seed, baking bread, going fishing. Jesus is speaking to country people in terms they could readily understand. This method is the essence of wise catechesis.

★

The first of these parables is the longest. Jesus describes the kingdom as being like a sower going out to scatter seed and what he says may indeed be read as a kind of examination of conscience. Everyone who has been baptised is called to be a sower of seed. The seed is the gospel message. As we go about our business, scattering seed, so to speak, where does the seed fall, what effect do our actions have? Some seed, Jesus says, is wasted. It falls, not into soil at all, but is dropped carelessly onto the path, and is eaten by birds. Other seed falls onto rocky ground. It springs up, but the soil there is too shallow and so what grows soon withers. Other seed falls among bram-bles and thistles, so that although it bears fruit, before long it is choked by the thorns and thistles and dies. And finally, there is seed that falls into rich soil that yields a fine harvest. It is not difficult to apply the image to our own behaviour.

As each one of us is called to sow the seed, how effective are we? At times I may be careless. Opportunities are lost. The seed I scatter is wasted, left by the wayside. Then, aren't there times when my behaviour is superficial, when I am caught up in sudden, trivial enthusiasms that don't last? What I do withers because my motives are shallow. And aren't there times as well when my intentions may be good and what I do may prove to be worthwhile, but all the same I find myself too preoccupied with other concerns, thorns and thistles that rise up and throttle the good that otherwise I might achieve? And then, I hope, there may be times when what I do, the seed I scatter, is sown in rich soil so that it does bear fruit, yielding a fine harvest. Each one of us is called to be a sower, so that the kingdom may come.

But we are not only the sower. We may listen to the parable and see ourselves also as the soil. Remember, the seed is the gospel message. How do I respond to it? Do I allow it to touch my heart? What kind of soil does the seed find in me? Am I so hard-hearted that it is wasted, ricocheting off my hard heart, not able to take root in it at all? Or, while the seed may fall into my heart and begin to grow, am I too superficial, too shallow for it to have much effect? Or perhaps, while the soil is good, are there too many thistles and thorns inside me – brambles that distract me from the good that otherwise might be accomplished? Or it may be that in my heart there is good soil that receives the seed of the gospel generously and bears fruit after all. Listening to the parable in this way, it occurs to me that I am like a landscape, sometimes hard and wasteful, sometimes superficial and shallow, sometimes well intentioned, but too easily distracted, and sometimes, I hope, generous enough to yield a harvest. May that harvest be at least reasonably rich.

Becoming kingdom, fulfilling the Father's will that his kingdom may come here on earth as in heaven, is an inspiring ideal. Enthusiasm for the kingdom could carry us away. The next parable, however, provides a check to that enthusiasm. It too is a parable about the sowing of seed.

Here the kingdom is compared to good seed that has been sown, but then, during the night, an enemy comes who sows bad seed among the good, so that weeds grow up in the harvest of wheat. The householder's servants are appalled and offer to go and remove the weeds so that the wheat may flourish. But the owner of the land tells them not to and explains his reason: 'for in gathering the weeds, you would uproot the wheat along with them'. We know we should do good and avoid evil, but reality is often complex.

Of course, we must not collude with evil, but we must also be alert to a kind of purist perfectionism that can cause harm. Moral controversies offer obvious examples. I recall a conversation long ago in Rome with a visiting archbishop who was lamenting how an opportunity had been lost in his country to reduce the number of weeks within which it was legal for an abortion to be carried out. An amendment before their parliament with a reasonable chance of success had been defeated because an extreme pro-life group would not support it. They felt it did not go far enough. They wanted total abolition and so would have felt compromised had they backed any measure that allowed for any abortion at all. Their intransigence, therefore, led not only to the defeat of the amendment, but also to a far more permissive outcome, abortion made legal up to birth. If the kingdom is to come alive, it may not be immediately obvious what is wheat and what is weed.

*

In 1990 I was again accompanying a group on pilgrimage in Israel. One morning, after crossing the sea of Galilee, we walked into Capernaum. I was bringing up the rear and our guide, Dudu Grinker, was out in front. Dudu was tall and bearded, a gifted teacher, imaginative and authoritative. I imagine Moses must have looked rather like Dudu. And suddenly he turned and called out to me, 'Father, come here.' I obeyed. As I approached him, he reached up and broke a pod from an overhanging branch. 'Hold out your hand,' he ordered. I did so. Then he cracked the pod and two small, black dots rolled onto my palm. 'What are those?' he asked. My mind went blank. 'They are mustard seeds,' he explained, 'and if you come in season, you will find this whole area covered with mustard trees.' The incident comes to mind whenever I think of the third of these parables of the kingdom in which Jesus told his followers that the kingdom was 'like a mustard seed that someone took and sowed in his field. It is the smallest of all the seeds, but when it has grown it is the greatest of shrubs and becomes a tree, so the birds of the air come and make nests in its branches.' From small beginnings vast consequences may come to pass.

The next parable makes, not the same, but a corresponding point. While small seeds cause many trees to grow so that large flocks of birds nest in their branches, a little yeast makes it possible for a woman to leaven three measures of dough. We may say that the effect of the seed is quantitative as many trees are grown, but the effect of the yeast is qualitative as the dough rises.

The following two parables also make a pair; at a glance they may seem merely repetitious. The first likens the kingdom to a treasure hidden in a field. The person who finds it is filled with joy when he discovers it, hides it again, and goes and sells everything he owns in order to buy the field where the treasure is hidden. Nothing is more precious than that treasure. In the second parable, it is not a treasure that is found, but 'one pearl of great value'. Here too, the merchant who has found it, like the man who found the treasure, goes and sells all that he has in order to buy the wondrous pearl. But there is an instructive difference. In the first parable, the kingdom of heaven, as I have mentioned, is like the treasure hidden in the field; but in the second, the kingdom is not likened to the pearl, but to 'a merchant in search of fine pearls'. The kingdom is infinitely precious, but so are those who go in search of such a treasure, even a single pearl of great value. They too are kingdom.

The final parable in the sequence shifts the focus from sowing seeds and baking bread and hidden treasure to the lakeside, although it has a link with the parable about wheat and weeds. The kingdom is now likened to a great net cast into the sea that captures fish of every kind. When the fish have been brought ashore, they need to be sorted out, the good from the bad. In due course, there is need for discernment. During the harvest, there was a time when we may not have been sure which was wheat and which was weed, but – changing the metaphor – there comes a time eventually when it is possible to separate what is good from what is bad.

★

This sequence of parables provides us with a vision of what it means to become kingdom. We are to be people who sow seeds and we should also ourselves be the soil into which the seed falls. The kingdom, however, will emerge only gradually and not in a way that is immediately perfect: there will be weeds among the wheat and we will have to be patient before we can separate the good from the bad, wheat from weeds, good fish from bad. Our first glimpse of the kingdom may well be in small things, like the mustard seed or the yeast, but we must never lose sight of the overwhelming truth that nothing is more precious than the kingdom, the treasure that may seem for a long time to be hidden from us. Nevertheless, like the merchant, we must keep on searching for the pearl of great price. It is through that relentless, steadfast search that we become kingdom. And let me add one final thought.

When reflecting on the first of these parables, the sower going out to sow, which I referred to as a kind of examination of conscience, I suggested, first of all, that we can identify with the sower. Are we careless or superficial, distracted or conscientious? I then suggested that we can also identify with the soil. Are we hard and unyielding, or shallow, or too preoccupied with other concerns, or are we rich soil that bears fruit? I described myself as a landscape. But besides identifying with the sower and the soil, I now want to suggest that we can identify with the seed as well. Sowing conscientiously and cultivating our hearts so as to receive the seed within ourselves as rich soil, we gradually become kingdom. In those words of Pope Paul VI that have been quoted so often, but that we must never forget, people today listen more willingly to witnesses than to teachers, and if they do listen to teachers, 'it is because they are witnesses'.[1] Like the merchant seeking tirelessly for the pearl of great price, we are transformed little by little into what we desire. How wise Jim Sullivan was to bring the kingdom into people. As witnesses, we become kingdom.

1 Pope St Paul VI, *Evangelii Nuntiandi*, n.41.

12

Showing mercy

When Cardinal Jorge Bergoglio, the Archbishop of Buenos Aires, had to visit Rome in years past, he stayed at the Casa del Clero, a Vatican residence in the Via della Scrofa. Nearby there is the French National Church, San Luigi dei Francesi, where in the Contarelli Chapel there are paintings of St Matthew by Caravaggio. One is of Matthew with an angel, the second depicts his martyrdom, but it may be that the most famous is the calling of Matthew by Jesus. Jesus' finger, pointing at the tax collector, reflects Michelangelo's finger of God the Father, creating Adam, in the Sistine Chapel. This painting of the Saviour calling the sinner captures a moment that has inspired Cardinal Bergoglio. It is said that he would often go and pray in that chapel.

On St Matthew's feast day, the Divine Office includes a reading from the homilies of the Venerable Bede (672–735). Bede was a monk of Jarrow in Northumberland. A Doctor of the Church, he is famous as a historian, a Scripture scholar, and for his writings about the saints. In this homily he wrote that, when Jesus looked at Matthew, 'he saw a tax collector, and since he looked at him in pity and choosing him as a disciple, he said, "Follow me".'[1] The reference to looking with pity and choosing seems perhaps rather laboured in English, but in the original Latin it is crisp, *Miserando atque Eligendo*. And that expression from Bede is Cardinal Bergoglio's episcopal motto

1 St Bede the Venerable, Homily 21, *The Divine Office* iii, p.278*.

Caravaggio, *The Calling of St Matthew*

and remained his motto after he was elected Pope in March 2013. When Jesus saw the despised tax collector, he looked on him with compassion, with mercy, and chose him. And showing mercy is fundamental to the ministry of Pope Francis.

On the Sunday following his election, when he spoke to the crowds in St Peter's Square before praying the Angelus, he insisted that there is no one beyond the reach of God's loving mercy. People may refuse the mercy, forgiveness and love they are being offered, but the offer is nonetheless being made to them. God never tires of forgiving, although, the Pope reminded those who had gathered, we sometimes grow weary of asking for forgiveness. We must not do that. There is no limit to divine mercy.

This truth is the bedrock of Christianity: there is no limit to divine mercy. The very idea lifts the heart. If a longing for the kingdom to come, as we have reflected, lies at the heart of the Lord's Prayer, that longing may be satisfied by creating what may be called a culture of forgiveness, first, through our accepting forgiveness for our own sins, our trespasses, by God and, secondly, by our forgiving those who have trespassed against us. Forgiveness is the fruit of mercy. To receive forgiveness is to be shown mercy. But we need to be wary. How often we look askance at the scribes and Pharisees who persecuted Jesus and tried to trick him, and we applaud the way Jesus sought the company of tax collectors and sinners. All the same, it is important to pause and take stock. It could be easy to be carried away and not notice the implications.

These tax collectors and sinners, Matthew himself, for example (Matthew 9:9), and the woman taken in adultery (John 8:1–11), were not just lovable rogues. They were people who were doing real harm to others. Jesus did not seek them out to collude with them, condoning the misery they caused. He sought them out to change them, calling Matthew to follow him and telling the woman to go away and not to sin anymore. If we are taking these matters seriously, we need to ask who might be the tax collectors and sinners of our own day.

The 'tax collectors' might be identified with those whose greed and arrogance, self-indulgence and extravagance, have squandered the savings of so many good people; the 'sinners' might be identified with those who have abused vulnerable people, whether young or old – physically, emotionally, sexually and psychologically. These are the people whom society regards with contempt. The tax collectors and sinners of Jesus' day are the embezzlers and abusers of ours. Can we bring ourselves to forgive them? That those whom they have damaged take priority goes without saying. Yet embezzlers and abusers need healing too. The demands of compassion are an immense challenge. No one is beyond the reach of divine mercy. Nor is there anyone not in need of it. We have to examine ourselves.

*

St Caesarius of Arles (470/1–543) may not be the saint best known to many people. He was bishop of Arles, not far from Marseille, for almost forty years. Nevertheless, in a sermon of extraordinary power and perception, he observed acutely that while everyone wishes to receive mercy, few are prepared to show it to others. Yet which of us is not in need of mercy? 'What effrontery,' he remarked, 'to want to receive what you neglect to give!' And he pointed out that there are two kinds of mercy, 'mercy on earth and mercy in heaven, human mercy and divine mercy'. Then he explained the distinction: 'What is human mercy like? It makes you concerned for the hardship of the poor. What is divine mercy like? It forgives sinners.' And he continued,

> In this world God is cold and hungry in all the poor, as he himself said: 'As you did it to one of the least of these my brethren, you did it to me.' God then is pleased to give from heaven, but he desires to receive on earth . . . Show mercy on earth, and you will receive mercy in heaven.[2]

When considering mercy, St Caesarius and Pope Francis seem to be of one mind.

Pope Francis's commitment to the ministry of mercy was made more evident on 11 April 2015 when he proclaimed an Extraordinary Jubilee Year. These Holy Years, as they are known, usually take place every twenty-five years, but there can be extraordinary Holy Years as well.[3] This Jubilee Year of

2 St Caesarius of Arles, Sermon 25, 1, *The Divine Office* iii, pp.354–5.
3 In 1983 Pope St John Paul II proclaimed such a year to mark the traditional anniversary of Jesus' crucifixion in AD 33 1950 years before.

Mercy was scheduled to begin on 8 December 2015, the fifti-
eth anniversary of the closing of the Second Vatican Council,
and the Pope's immediate emphasis was on mercy, quoting the
words of Pope St John XXIII at its opening, that the Church
'wishes to use the medicine of mercy rather than taking up
arms of severity'.[4] Indeed, the document announcing this
special year was called *Misericordiae Vultus*, that is *The Face of
Mercy*. Within it, three crucial points in particular can be
identified.

★

Jesus Christ is the face of the Father's mercy (n.1)

The most memorable homily I have ever heard on 8 December,
the feast of the Immaculate Conception, was preached by
Abbot Timothy Wright, a former abbot of Ampleforth. After
completing his time as abbot, he had come to Rome and had
then joined the staff at the Beda College as one of our spiritual
directors, helping the students to discern and prepare for their
ordination as priests. On this occasion, he spoke simply, reflecting on three words: problem, solution and fulfilment. The
problem, of course, was original sin – the sin of Adam, that
handicapped humanity; the solution was God sending his son
born of a woman; and the fulfilment of that solution was Mary's
response to the angel's invitation, 'Behold, the handmaid of the
Lord. Let it be done to me according to your word.' It was
unforgettable. Jesus, the Son of God and the son of Mary, was
the face of the Father's mercy, lavished on humanity.

At the heart of this mystery of salvation is Jesus who is
perfectly faithful in love, in his love for his Father and in his
love for the human race. As we recognised during Passiontide,
his faithful love for his Father meant that he was perfectly

4 *Misericordiae Vultus*, n.4.

obedient to his Father's will and his faithful love for humanity meant that he was perfectly at the service of our need. What the Father willed was for us to be reconciled to him, and our deepest need was for that reconciliation. There is, therefore, as we have seen, this perfect correspondence between the Father's will and our human need. And Jesus seeks to bring about our salvation by revealing his unlimited love for us, even to the point of dying on the cross, so that this overwhelming love of his may open our eyes, our hearts and our minds by revealing to us the Father's love. Jesus is the face of the Father's loving mercy.

Throughout Jesus' ministry that loving mercy is on display. He sees crowds that seem lost, like sheep without a shepherd, and has compassion on them and teaches them (Matthew 9:36); moved by compassion, he heals those who are sick (Matthew 14:14); when a large crowd listens to him, staying with him for days, he will not just send them away, but again, out of compassion, makes sure that first they are fed (Matthew 15:32). Jesus sees a widow, taking her son to be buried and, once more, moved by compassion, restores him to life (Luke 7:13). When he has healed the Gerasene demoniac, Jesus was asked by the man who had been possessed if he might stay with him, but Jesus sends him home, instructing him to tell his friends 'how much the Lord has done for you, and what mercy he has shown you' (Mark 5:19). And he tells parables about one sheep in a flock of a hundred being lost, but found, about a woman with ten silver coins finding the one that was lost, and famously about the prodigal son 'who was lost and has been found' (Luke 15). All three give cause for rejoicing. And he tells Peter that forgiveness is not to be measured out, granted just seven times but seventy-seven times (Matthew 18:21–2). There is no limit to the mercy we receive so there should be no limit to the mercy we should show.

By his teaching and his actions Jesus shows that there should be no end to forgiveness. He is the face of the Father's mercy, and his face should be reflected by the Church.

Mercy is the very foundation of the Church's life (n.10)

'The Church's very credibility,' Pope Francis emphasised, as he announced the Holy Year, 'is seen in how she shows merciful and compassionate love.'[5] To be 'merciful like the Father' became the motto for this Holy Year.[6] 'Be merciful just as your Father is merciful', Jesus declared in Luke's Gospel (Luke 6:36). What does that mean for the Church, for those who try to follow Jesus? It means, first of all, if we recall the teaching of St Francis de Sales, that we should always be on the watch for the good in people. And then it makes sense to recall the Pope's encouragement to those who had gathered for World Youth Day in Rio de Janeiro in 2013, when he begged them from the bottom of his heart, to read the Beatitudes and to read Matthew 25. We have been here before, but repetition is often worthwhile.[7] One benefit of Ordinary Time is to return to key points like this, ponder them afresh and weave them into our understanding. I must confess, however, that it took me a while to appreciate the value of repetition.

When I first began to become familiar with the *Spiritual Exercises* of St Ignatius Loyola, there were meditations on Gospel passages that I found uplifting, but there were others that I found dry and difficult. It was a struggle to be faithful to the hour that I was supposed to spend meditating on some of them and frankly it was a relief when the hour was up. Then, that evening or the following day, I would turn to the next passage only to discover to my dismay that I was instructed simply to repeat what I had just completed. Repeat! I felt I had sucked all the blood out of that stone that I possibly could. Now I smile at my alarm. Experience has taught me the value of repetition. A return visit uncovers further depths. And so it is here.

5 *Misericordiae Vultus*, n.10.
6 *Misericordiae Vultus*, n.14.
7 See Chapter 5, 'Being ordinary', see above, p.58.

We have to remember that the Beatitudes are not an exhaustive summary of Christian teaching, but guides, and they include, of course, the reference to mercy: 'Blessed are the merciful, for they will receive mercy.' They *will* receive mercy, so something for the future, not something immediate. They may be persecuted for righteousness' sake, but they shall have mercy shown them.

Blessed too, we are told, are the poor in spirit. Poverty of spirit indicates a detachment from material possessions, generosity of heart. Remember the rich young man who comes to Jesus, asking what he must do to gain eternal life. And Jesus tells him to keep the commandments, not to murder or commit adultery, not to steal or bear false witness, and to honour his father and mother and love his neighbour. And the young man declares he has done all that. He wants to know what he must do in order to be perfect. He is not a bad man, probably rather a good one; but it seems he is quite full of himself. In Australia he would probably be regarded as a tall poppy. And Jesus then tells him that, if he wants to be perfect, he must go and sell all that he has and come back and follow him. And the young man goes away sad, because he has many possessions. What Jesus asks of him is more than he can manage, though I've wondered from time to time whether he returned later. I like to think that he did. But the immediate demand was too much for him to bear (Matthew 19:16–22).

Reflecting on this call to poverty of spirit, to generosity of heart, it is necessary to realise that Jesus' instruction to the rich young man has implications for all Christians. Jesus' words, 'Go and sell; come and follow,' are not to be understood as some absolute ideal that everyone ought to follow, an ideal that exalts destitution. The Gerasene demoniac, for example, released from possession, wanted, as we have seen, to join Jesus, to follow him, but was told that for him that wasn't necessary. His vocation was to return home and tell his friends what had been done for him and the mercy he had been shown. The challenge for the rich young man, however, was different. It was not a call to some absolute ideal, but the challenge that would confront him at the point where he was most vulnerable. He thought he could do anything, but the tall poppy needed to be trimmed. He was more attached to his wealth than he realised. That took priority. And similarly the challenge for the Church, seeking to be merciful, is to recognise that that is where the Lord will challenge us as well, putting his finger on our weaknesses, revealing our vulnerability.

And so we turn to Matthew 25. Will we carry out what are known as the corporal works of mercy? Will we feed the hungry, give drink to the thirsty, welcome the stranger, clothe the naked, and visit those who are sick or in prison? Will we care for those who are in need? And will we exercise the spiritual works of mercy as well? That can be particularly testing. It could be easy to appear superior or condescending, making us more like the rich young man who initially imagined that nothing was beyond him. What I find significant about the works of mercy we call spiritual, however, is the way they are actually rooted in human sensitivity and maturity.

The historical example that stands out for me is the occasion when Augustine went to Milan and met there the bishop, Ambrose. It was a critical moment in Augustine's gradual conversion to Christianity. He and Ambrose, with Gregory the Great and Jerome, have come to be recognised as the four great Fathers of the Latin Church. But, when Augustine and Ambrose met, what was it that impressed Augustine about Ambrose? Was it the force of Ambrose's arguments? Did these two great minds engage with each other and did the strength of the case Ambrose presented win Augustine over? Not at all. 'I began to like him,' Augustine wrote later, 'at first indeed not as a teacher of the truth, for I had absolutely no confidence in your Church, but as a human being who was kind to me.'[8]

8 Augustine, *Confessions* V. xiii (23), tr. Henry Chadwick, (Oxford, Oxford University Press, 1991), p.88.

What moved Augustine was the kindness he was shown. Do we underestimate too easily the worth of human qualities like courtesy, thoughtfulness, consideration, understanding and kindness? They can shape the way we show mercy.

So, will we be gentle and compassionate with those who are anxious, shrouded in doubt and darkness, or lost in loneliness? Will we find a way to help people make sense of the gospel message which, until then, has been to them a closed book and meaningless? Will we look for ways to comfort those who are grieving, perhaps by our patient, silent presence, more than by anything we have to say? How often words in those circumstances provide no answer at all. Will we pray for those who ask for our prayers and not forget to pray for those who have no one else to pray for them? We cannot be expected to remember everyone by name, but we can maintain a general intention to pray each day for those who have asked for our prayers. And when we ourselves have been wronged or misjudged, will we forgive those who have harmed us? In such ways, will we by our way of living, however inadequate we may feel it to be, strive nevertheless like Jesus to reflect the face of the Father's mercy, so as to be merciful as the Father is merciful? If we do, we shall be learning from Caesarius of Arles. By recognising our own need for mercy and giving thanks for the mercy we have received, we will be led to show mercy to others. That mercy is the very foundation of the Church's life.

Pilgrimage (n.14)

Becoming kingdom, showing mercy, it will be obvious, does not take place instantaneously. Holy Years are times of pilgrimage. Announcing the Year of Mercy, Pope Francis explained, 'The practice of *pilgrimage* has a special place in the Holy Year, because it represents the journey each of us makes in this life.

Life itself is a pilgrimage, and the human being is a *viator*, a pilgrim travelling along the road, making his way to the desired destination.'⁹ We are journeying into light and the journey can be demanding.

The focal point for pilgrims to Rome during these Holy Years is to visit one of the Papal basilicas and pray there. They enter through the Holy Door, a door that is otherwise sealed and opened only during these Jubilee Years. One friend of mine who happened to be in Rome during the Jubilee Year in 2000, told me about her experience when she decided to go through the Holy Door in the basilica near where she was staying. Standing outside, preparing herself to enter, she felt suddenly overcome with emotion, and then by chance an acquaintance came past her, tapped her lightly on the shoulder and said cheerily, 'Come on in,' as he strolled casually through. But she stood there still and wept. Eventually she felt ready to enter. When pilgrimage is taken seriously, it can be demanding.

There is a particular hazard along the pilgrim path that can be seen as the apparent clash between mercy and justice. If God is merciful, for ever disregarding evil, how can he be just? But if he is just, how can he be merciful? It may be, however, that this dilemma is misconceived. For a certain cast of mind, of course – the cast of mind that seeks precision, clarity and security – the dilemma will be self-evident. But another cast of mind will view the matter differently, not seeing justice and mercy as irreconcilable alternatives. While we measure out justice cautiously, often meagrely, God dispenses mercy lavishly. As Pope Francis observed pithily, 'Mercy is not opposed to justice, but rather expresses God's way of reaching out to the sinner, offering him a new chance to look at himself, convert, and believe.' And he quoted a remark, typical of St Augustine:

9 *Misericordiae Vultus*, n.14.

'It is easier for God to hold back anger than mercy.'[10] God's initiative is more gracious than we can imagine.

In all societies there are contrasting casts of mind. The Church is no different. Throughout what the Jesuit historian, John O'Malley, has called the long nineteenth century which can be said to have lasted from the French Revolution till the death of Pope Pius XII in 1958, the dominant Catholic cast of mind had been static, characterised by its desire for security, rooted in precise definition.[11] Yet by the time the Council opened in 1962, awareness had emerged of the need for an alternative. In its Constitution on the Church in the Modern World, *Gaudium et Spes*, a shift was recognised: 'The human race is moving from a more static view of things to one which is more dynamic and evolutionary, giving rise to new combinations of problems which call for new analyses and syntheses.'[12] Making such a statement, of course, does not mean that all its implications were recognised. That has come later, more gradually, and it continues. And furthermore, to recognise a process, something dynamic, instead of settling for a setting that is static, cut and dried, is not a way of welcoming indiscipline and laxity; it is rather a way of reaching out to those trapped in a kind of cul-de-sac and offering them a fresh opportunity to know themselves better, to pursue a new path and journey on towards the light.

*

One further parable of the kingdom may illustrate the connection between justice and mercy and bring it into focus more helpfully.

In Matthew's Gospel, Jesus speaks about a landowner who needed people to work in his vineyard. Early one morning the

10 *Misericordiae Vultus*, n.21; see Augustine, *Sermons on the Psalms*, 76, 11.
11 See John W. O'Malley, *What Happened at Vatican II*, (London, Harvard University Press, 2008), pp.53–92.
12 *Gaudium et Spes*, n.5.

landowner finds some workers, agrees with them what they will be paid for their day's labour and sends them off to work. At various times during the day he comes across others seeking work and employs them as well. Even at the eleventh hour he finds still more who have had no work all day and he sends them too to work in the vineyard. Then at the end of the day he pays all his workers. He begins by paying those whom he had hired most recently and he pays them the daily wage that he had agreed with those whom he had employed first. These, therefore, hope for more and, when they don't get it, they complain that they have been treated unfairly, as they have had to bear the heat of the day. But the landowner is unmoved. He tells them that they have received what had been agreed. 'Are you envious,' he asks them, 'because I am generous?' (Matthew 20:1–16). Mercy embraces justice, but also reaches beyond it, as Pope Francis made clear when he reflected on their relationship in *Misericordiae Vultus*. He spoke there of mercy and justice, not as 'two contradictory realities, but two dimensions of a single reality that unfolds progressively until it culminates in the fullness of love'.[13]

13 See *Misericordiae Vultus*, n.20.

13

Reforming the Church

In 1206 a young man in Umbria, Francesco Bernardone, was coming to realise that his life needed to take a new direction. Francesco, now known famously as Francis of Assisi, was praying one day before a crucifix in the dilapidated church of San Damiano and it seemed to him that the figure on the cross was speaking to him, instructing him to rebuild the church. At first he imagined that he was being asked to rebuild that church, San Damiano, that was old and in disrepair to the point of collapse. But the reality was far greater. Francis and the companions that gathered around him came, of course, to be known as Franciscans, and like others at that time, Dominicans and Carmelites, were to spearhead the rebuilding and renewing of the Church at large.[1] Renewal had been needed before and it would be needed again, more than once.

Three hundred years later, the Church was obviously in dire straits once more. Martin Luther's Ninety-Five Theses, nailed to the door of the Wittenburg Castle Church, were a call to debate contentious issues in the Church at that time, but his act has come to be seen as the trigger that provoked the sixteenth century Protestant Reformation. Rome's response to Luther and the controversies of those years was eventually formulated at the Council of Trent (1545–63) whose documents

1 For more information, see Maurice Carmody, *The Franciscan Story*, (London, Athena Press, 2008).

The San Damiano Crucifix

were regarded as a blueprint for the Counter-Reformation. Changes, of course, still occurred, but increasingly the Catholic outlook came to be more and more static. And, in particular, as fresh developments – both political and intellectual – emerged during the Enlightenment in the nineteenth century, Rome itself became ever more defensive, entering that long nineteenth century from 1789 to 1958.

Throughout that period, the idea that the Church might need to be renewed, indeed reformed, was seen as virtually a contradiction in terms. When Archbishop Angelo Roncalli, the papal nuncio in Paris, heard about a book by the Dominican theologian, Yves Congar, called, *True and False Reform in the Church*, he was astonished. Reform of the Church, he asked himself, how is that possible?[2] But some years later, in 1958, that same Angelo Roncalli was elected Pope and took the name John XXIII. Then within months of his election he had announced the calling of the Second Vatican Council and set in motion the process of reform with which the Church is still and will always be engaged. As the Council's Constitution on the Church, *Lumen Gentium* (*The Light of the Nations*), was to declare, the Church 'is at one and the same time holy and always in need of purification'.[3] When the Council opened on 11 October 1962, in words that have been quoted often, Pope John stated plainly, 'For the deposit of faith itself is one thing, and the way in which it is expressed is another.'[4]

2 See Fergus Kerr, *Twentieth-Century Catholic Theologians*, (Oxford, Blackwells, 2007), p.36.
3 *Lumen Gentium*, n.8.
4 For an account of this speech, see Peter Hebblethwaite, *John XXIII, Pope of the Council*, (London, Geoffrey Chapman, 1984), pp.430–3, and O'Malley, *What happened at Vatican II*, pp.94–6.

Pope John died at Pentecost the following year, 3 June 1963. The new Pope, Cardinal Giovanni Battista Montini, the Archbishop of Milan, became Pope Paul VI and assumed responsibility for bringing the Council to its conclusion. It took three further sessions. As the work of the Council involved change, there were inevitable tensions, clashes especially between those with differing casts of mind, some opposed to change altogether, others unabashed enthusiasts for it. But, in any case, change takes time. Pope Paul's particular concern was to achieve as great a unanimity for the Council's decisions as possible. It was not a recipe for personal popularity, but to a remarkable degree he achieved that goal. When he died in 1978, the cardinals elected as his successor the lovable Patriarch of Venice, Cardinal Albino Luciani. Luciani as Pope decided to be called after his two immediate predecessors and so became Pope John Paul I. He died just thirty-three days later, to be succeeded by the first non-Italian Pope for more than four hundred and fifty years, Cardinal Karol Wojtyla, the Archbishop of Cracow, who, not least out of respect for Luciani, became Pope John Paul II.

John Paul was Pope for more than twenty-six years and during that time he travelled extensively. He carried out as well an exceptional programme in preparation for the Jubilee Year of 2000, bringing bishops to Rome from every continent for individual synods to reflect on their needs for the new millennium. He was greatly admired and loved by many. When he died on Easter Saturday 2005, I happened to be in Dublin, but I was returning to Rome the following day and, on arrival, I went at once to St Peter's Square. There were groups gathered, some singing, some praying, some silent. A sadness hung in the air, a sense of absence which you could almost touch. Although this pilgrim Pope had often been absent on those travels, now he was absent in a different way. To be present at his funeral some days later was an incomparable privilege. And besides his tireless travels he had also produced an extraordinary range of writings that took their inspiration from Pope John's Council. Nevertheless, the Council's work was still not over. I believe it helps, when pondering how the Church might be renewed, to be aware, however sketchily, of this background and bear it in mind.

★

The Pope who succeeded John Paul was, of course, Cardinal Joseph Ratzinger who took the name Benedict XVI. As a young man, Ratzinger had had a reputation for being a gifted and imaginative theologian. He had been one of the theological experts at Vatican II. Since 1981, however, he had been the Cardinal Prefect of the Congregation for the Doctrine of the Faith where, in spite of his unfailing personal courtesy, he had gained a reputation as a stern enforcer of doctrinal orthodoxy. After his election as Pope, people were wondering which personality would emerge, the theologian or the enforcer. And the wisest answer to that question, it seems to me, came from Cardinal Cormac at a press conference that I was fortunate enough to attend at the English College in Rome after the Pope's inaugural mass.

When the question of the Pope's character was raised, the Cardinal replied that it was not a question of contrasting the theologian and the Prefect and wondering which of them was the more authentic, but of recognising that both represented responsibilities which the former theologian and the former Cardinal Prefect had had to undertake. It was not a matter, therefore, of choosing between them. They were more like two chapters in a life story. And now a third had begun. Pope Benedict would be different again.[5] As indeed he was.

One evident sign of that difference emerged later that year, in December. Before Christmas it is customary for the

5 See *The Tablet*, 23 April 2005, p.36.

Pope to address members of the Roman Curia. It is an opportunity for him to thank them for their work and to wish them the blessings of the feast. It is also an opportunity to reflect on the year that has passed. So it was natural for Benedict to recall the death of his predecessor. He also spoke about World Youth Day that he had attended in Cologne and the Synod on the Eucharist that had been held in Rome that autumn. And then he moved on to one further, intriguing topic.

That year, 2005, was the fortieth anniversary of the end of the Second Vatican Council, and the Pope asked what had been achieved during those years and why implementing the Council's teaching had been so difficult. He identified the key issue as hermeneutical, that is to say, as one of interpretation. There were those who interpreted what they saw as the true spirit of the Council as a break with the past. They followed what he called a hermeneutic of rupture that dismissed and wished to abandon much that had gone before. And there were others who interpreted the Council's work in continuity with the past, who pursued, in other words, a hermeneutic of reform. This was the path that Benedict affirmed as authentic. At the same time, he acknowledged that what Pope John had proposed was demanding, on the one hand, being true to the Church's teaching, the deposit that has been revealed, while, on the other, presenting it afresh.

Later in the address he moved on from the stark contrast between rupture and continuity and spoke explicitly of reform, a notion that even in the 1950s had aroused fierce hostility in Rome at the Holy Office (as it was then known).[6] John O'Malley, analysing it from a historical viewpoint, has made it plain, however, that Pope Benedict's address 'powerfully rehabilitated' the notion. He

6 Yves Congar had been forbidden to have his book on reform reprinted or translated. The Holy Office is now the Congregation for the Doctrine of the Faith.

also called the Pope's description of reform one that it was difficult to improve upon. It was the point where the Pope stated that it is precisely in the 'blending of continuity and discontinuity at different levels that the very nature of true reform consists'.[7]

*

Change is often challenging. Blending continuity and discontinuity in the service of reforming the Church is a delicate process. John O'Malley has pinpointed invaluably three particular terms, distinct but overlapping, that were integral to that process. The first was *aggiornamento*, an Italian word for modernising, not in the pejorative sense, but in the sense of bringing up to date. When opening the Council and insisting on adherence to the Church's teaching 'in its entirety and preciseness', Pope John had also affirmed that this teaching 'should be studied and expounded through the methods of research and through the literary forms of modern thought'. It was the passage leading up to his distinction between the deposit of faith, on the one hand, and the way it is presented, on the other, and it was quoted by Pope Benedict in his address to the Roman Curia. The second term was development. *Aggiornamento*, what is brought up to date, implies an openness to the possibility of teaching unfolding, progressing, developing. When John Henry Newman was agonising over whether the Roman Church was indeed the Catholic Church and whether he should, therefore, be received into it, the crucial impediment for him was teaching that he had regarded previously as added by Rome to the deposit of faith, such as certain Marian doctrines and teaching on Purgatory. His dilemma was resolved when he came to recognise truth as

---

7 John W. O'Malley, '"The Hermeneutic of Reform": A Historical Analysis', *Theological Studies* 73 (2012), pp.517-46: quotation of Pope Benedict, p.543. See Pope Benedict XVI, 'Christmas Address to the Roman Curia', 22 December 2005.

alive so that, as time passes, it develops, becoming more equable, purer, and stronger.[8] And the third term is *ressourcement*, a French word, expressing a return to the sources. When doctrine is developed, how can the development be known as authentic? One key criterion will be by investigating its origins and discovering the harmony between those origins and what has emerged. None of these three terms was entirely novel. What made them exceptional, however, during the Second Vatican Council was how pervasive they were in the debates and discussions and how profound was their influence.[9]

One plain consequence of that influence is evident in the way language was used. It revealed the different casts of mind that were in play. The shift in style indicated, as O'Malley noted, 'almost two different visions of Catholicism'. And he went on at some length to offer illustrations of this shift:

From commands to invitations, from laws to ideals, from definition to mystery, from threats to persuasion, from coercion to conscience, from monologue to dialogue, from ruling to serving, from withdrawn to integrated, from vertical to horizontal, from exclusion to inclusion, from hostility to friendship, from rivalry to partnership, from suspicion to trust, from static to ongoing, from passive acceptance to active engagement, from fault-finding to appreciation, from prescriptive to principled, from behavior modification to inner appropriation'.[10]

8 See J. H. Newman, *An Essay on the Development of Christian Doctrine*, uniform edition, (Maryland, Christian Classics Inc., 1968), p.40.
9 See O'Malley, *What Happened at Vatican II*, pp.36–43, and *passim*. This brief summary in no way does justice to O'Malley's account to which I am indebted.
10 O'Malley, *What Happened at Vatican II*, p.307.

This was the vision that the Council embraced. It was not repudiating hierarchy or the need at times for authoritative decisions to be made; that would make no sense; but as a pastoral council it was seeking to moderate and balance an emphasis that for a long while had held sway and gone unchecked. In this way it was seeking to reform and renew the Church. And it is that vision that Pope Francis has been trying to make real. It has not been straightforward.

★

In 1873 Newman preached a sermon called, 'The Infidelity of the Future'. At one point he observed, 'With a whole population able to read, with cheap newspapers day by day conveying the news . . . , it is plain that we are at the mercy of even one unworthy member or false brother.'[11] There has, we now know, been many more than one. A devastating obstacle to the realising of the Council's vision has been the scandal of clerical sexual abuse that has been uncovered in the Church, serial abuse, children and vulnerable teenagers and adults groomed, lured into bed, raped or forced to perform oral sex, or to engage in degrading sexual acts. And besides sexual abuse, evidence has emerged of physical and psychological abuse as well. The discovery of this behaviour appals us. That the young or anyone who is vulnerable should be treated in such ways is sickening. We grieve for the survivors and victims and, as a priest myself, tarnished by association, humbly ask for pardon. Trust is a significant feature of any healthy personal relationship. It can take long to establish, and it can be destroyed in an instant.

Some years ago, the journalist, Nicholas Wapshott, commented upon the change in the way priests have come to be perceived: 'The figure of the saintly, benign counsellor, a

11 J. H. Newman, *Catholic Sermons*, (London, Burns & Oates, 1957), p.129.

comforting presence in times of distress, a resolute ally in the face of danger, is giving way to a quite different image – a cunning and deceitful deviant.'[12] These words make me think of a priest I know who was visiting his local supermarket one day. As he was entering, he held the door open courteously for a woman, unknown to him, who was leaving, carrying her shopping. She paused in front of him, spat in his face and told him, 'People like you should be in hell.' There has indeed been many more than one unworthy brother, to echo Newman, but there have also been many more, the vast majority like that man, who have sought to live their lives generously and faithfully, and have suffered because trust has broken down. How could such a situation have occurred?

There are people, of course, who regard the horror of sexual abuse in the Catholic Church as systemic, something integral to its way of life. And they readily point an accusing finger at the commitment made by religious priests to celibacy. But that analysis is lazy. There is not the space here to supply an adequate alternative and any attempt could be dismissed as defending the institution at the expense of survivors. That is not my intention. But one observation may nevertheless be worthwhile.

Celibacy in the Church has indeed been demanded and upheld rigorously in the past, even though there have always been those who, in spite of their commitment, have lapsed. What was largely lacking, however, for those entering ministerial priesthood or the religious life was the help people needed to develop affective maturity. Too many coped with their sexuality by repressing their feelings. They became uptight. Celibacy was seen as a discipline and they placed themselves under its control. And, come the sexual revolution of the 1960s and 1970s, when attitudes became more

12 Nicholas Wapshott, 'How the neighbourhood priest was betrayed by lies and lust', *The Times*, 7 December 2002.

permissive and discipline at large came to be eased, emotion and affectivity came to be valued, and there were those who had been holding their emotions in check, but who now felt able to relax. Much of that was good and healthy, but all the same there were also those in the Church who, having repressed their emotions and lacking affective maturity, although without realising it (who ever admits to it?) now felt liberated, but could not control their behaviour. And what damage they have done.

When trust has been lost, how can it be restored? How can the Church be renewed?

★

Reform, renewal, the restoration of trust, is not achieved by neat, clear, precise measures. Something better is needed than a slick routine. We have to reflect carefully on the nature of the Church, to explore our understanding of the Church. How we describe it is revealing. Do we speak of it as defensive, exclusive, static and inflexible? Or do we prefer to see it as open, inclusive, dynamic and developing? The adjectives we use tell a tale. An understanding of the Church has indeed developed in more recent decades. Three particular dates are noteworthy. They occur coincidentally at twenty-one year intervals.

First of all, in 1943, Pope Pius XII produced an encyclical letter on the Church, *Mystici Corporis* (*The Mystical Body of Christ*). It was seen as a breakthrough because of its use of Scripture. 'That the Church is a Body,' the Pope declared, 'we find asserted again and again in the Sacred Scriptures' (n.14), and he quoted the letter to the Romans, 'We who are many, are one body in Christ' (Romans 12:5). All the same, in spite of such biblical references, the Church was presented triumphantly as to be identified exclusively with the Roman Catholic Church, priority was placed on its legal structure, and, while the Pope spoke warmly of all the baptised, those with power in the Church, the clergy, were awarded pride of place. And this image of the Church, triumphalist, juridical, and clerical, was the image presented in the draft document on the Church that was put before the bishops at the Second Vatican Council and debated on 2 December 1962. However, later that morning Bishop Emile-Joseph De Smedt of Bruges addressed the gathering and denounced the draft on those very grounds, triumphalism, legalism and clericalism. It has been regarded as one of the most powerful and effective speeches of the Council. 'No mother,' De Smedt concluded, 'ever spoke in this way.'[13] The vast majority of those listening to him agreed.

The second date, therefore, occurred two years later, in 1964, twenty-one years after Pope Pius's encyclical. After long debate, the Dogmatic Constitution on the Church, *Lumen Gentum*, that was presented to the bishops for their vote on 21 November bore a very different character. Now the scriptural images for the Church were in full flood: the Church is a sheepfold, a field to be cultivated, a vineyard; it is a building, God's household in which God's family lives, God's dwelling and temple; and the temple is the holy city, the new Jerusalem, prepared like a bride to meet her husband; moreover, the Church is mother and spotless spouse (*Lumen Gentium*, n.6). And there is much more. Then this unique Church of Christ, organised in the world as a society and governed by the successor of Peter and the bishops in communion with him, was declared to *subsist in* the Catholic Church. Although the concept has caused considerable theological debate, 'subsistence' has been recognised generally as avoiding any oversimple and exclusive identification of the Church as the Catholic Church. Indeed, the document immediately goes on to state that outside the structure of the

13 See Peter Hebblethwaite, *John XXIII, Pope of the Council,* (London, Geoffrey Chapman, 1984), pp.459-60.

Church elements of sanctification and truth are to be found that impel towards Catholic unity (*Lumen Gentium* n.8). And then the principal image for the Church was affirmed as the people of God (*Lumen Gentium* nn.9–17), and only after that was attention paid to the Church's hierarchy. Here then was a vision of the Church that was biblical, inclusive, and not primarily hierarchical.

Balancing images is a delicate business. In 1984, the distinguished biblical scholar, Raymond Brown, observed: 'Within Roman Catholicism, if we have another decade of the dominance of people of God imagery, the body of Christ motif will need to re-emerge.' Here was a real challenge because the 'body of Christ' motif tended still to be associated with the legalism of Pius XII. But Brown was not trying to retrieve that past. As he explained a little later, his reason was 'to preserve a sense of a church holiness that comes from Christ and goes beyond the status of its members'.[14] Left unqualified, the image of 'the people of God' might be interpreted merely in an external way, but allied to a sense of the Church as the body of Christ something interior was also being affirmed, the Church's distinctive relationship with the Christ. And indeed the following year, 1985, twenty-one years after the promulgation of *Lumen Gentium*, an Extraordinary Synod was held in Rome to mark the anniversary of the ending of the Council in 1965. In its final report it declared, 'The ecclesiology of communion is a central and fundamental idea in the documents of the Council.'[15] So the breakthrough in 1943 was developed at the Council in 1964 and further refined in 1985.

Much has been written about the Church as communion, but the power of this vision lies particularly in the way it

14 Raymond E. Brown, *The Churches the Apostles Left Behind*, (London, Geoffrey Chapman, 1984), pp.60, 74.
15 *Synod Final Report* II, C. 1, (London, Catholic Truth Society, 1986), p.15.

combines three essential factors. First of all, those in communion are united. They are one. Secondly, however, recognising them as communion means acknowledging that their unity is not monolithic. Within the unity, the parts are diverse and distinctive. And, thirdly, those distinct parts are found to be in united communion by their relationship with one another. Here, therefore, is a way of understanding the Church that mirrors the Trinity: one God, three distinct persons, the unity and distinctiveness resolved by relationship. And it is this vision of the Church as communion that Pope Francis is trying to make real, most notably in his concern to clarify the relationship between the Roman centre of the Catholic Church and the integrity of the dioceses in communion with Rome throughout the world.

This issue became evident during the two synods on married life and the family in 2014 and 2015. One day, for example, Bishop Johan Bonny of Antwerp in Belgium made a plea for certain pastoral decisions to be referred to local bishops. The following day the same question was raised with Archbishop Mark Coleridge of Brisbane in an interview. The Archbishop agreed: 'The Pope has pointed in this direction by allowing some things to be referred to the local bishop. I think in Pope Francis's mind he would like to see a decentralisation where more authority is passed to the local bishop or the Bishops' Conference.'[16]

Pope Francis's viewpoint is giving priority to communion rather than hierarchy. There are those who see those two concepts on a collision course, but it need not be so. They may be incompatible when hierarchy is dominant and so creates demarcation disputes: who has responsibility for what, Rome or the local church? But when communion has priority, when we begin from unity, from what we have in

16 See https://brisbanecatholic.org.au/articles/on-the-road-together-some-questions-and-answers/, 8 October 2015 (accessed 13 May 2021).

common, then hierarchy finds its true place as the servant of communion, holding it together, in a happy phrase, 'like the membranes in a leaf'.[17]

*

To restore trust in the Church is no easy matter. Let me offer three suggestions for consideration, focusing on desire, maturity, and the way power is exercised. Of course, they are not exhaustive, but they may help us make a start.

Desire

Gerry Hughes was a Jesuit priest, a gifted spiritual director and a writer. He died, aged 90, in 2014. His best-known book is *God of Surprises*, which offers a path through St Ignatius' *Spiritual Exercises*, but in a later book, *God in All Things*, he makes a striking observation: 'I have never met anyone who could remember being taught the importance of desire. On the contrary, desire has usually been presented as a dangerous tendency; something to be curbed and brought into submission to "the will of God", which is the only legitimate desire for a conscientious Christian.' In other words, he is arguing that it is a mistake to assume that what we desire is necessarily at odds with what God desires for us. On the contrary, what God desires for us is our happiness, our delight, our joy. And so, he goes on, 'If we could discover what we really desire, we should have found God's will: if we could really find our true self, we should have found God.'[18]

17 Working Party on Collaborative Ministry, *The Sign We Give*, (Bishops' Conference of England and Wales, 1995), p.21.
18 Gerard W. Hughes, *God in All Things*, (London, Hodder & Stoughton, 2003), pp.73, 75.

This desire is evidently not wilful selfishness. We have met it already when reflecting on its place in prayer. When we are praying, what is it that we really want? In the depths of our being, in our heart of hearts, what is it that we most desire?[19] Think of Mother Teresa's desire not to build grand hospitals so that everyone in need would be cured. Such a plan could never be achieved. How can everyone be cured, how could disease be totally eradicated in our world? No, her desire was rather to bear witness to God's love for everyone, however desolate their condition, beginning with the homeless and the destitute, the sick and the dying on the streets of Kolkata. When, like her, we discover what we truly desire, we discover God's will for us.

Maturity

Maturity is a matter of balance. Wise parents, for example, people who are mature, accept their responsibilities for their children as parents, while allowing others, such as teachers caring for their children at school or university, and in due course their children themselves, to exercise their own proper responsibility as well. But those who are immature are either feckless, not bothering to give their children the support and help they need, or obsessively intrusive. An American friend who teaches at a university in the United States, told me of an occasion when a student was reported as missing. His mother phoned security and the university's president and a major search was soon under way. Happily he was found before too long. He was in the bar having a drink with friends, but had left his phone in his room. His mother had called him and, when he didn't reply, had panicked. Bewildered, he asked my friend, 'What have I

19 See, Chapter 6 'Lent: With Christ in the Wilderness', above, p.80.

done wrong?' 'You haven't done anything wrong,' my friend reassured him. 'It's just that you've left home, but your mother hasn't realised it yet.' Helicopter parents display immaturity by not allowing their children to take responsibility for themselves. Maturity involves accepting and allowing responsibility as appropriate.

A properly mature relationship between the Church and the world, therefore, would avoid the two extremes, neither maintaining indifference to the world, refusing to accept its proper responsibilities to the world, nor imposing itself theocratically on the world, as though the world had no distinct identity or value. Here too we recognise the pattern of the incarnation. As divine and human natures are distinct in the Christ, but united by relationship, so the Church and the world are distinct, but united by virtue of their relationship. In an article, published first in 1968, the German theologian, Karl Rahner, observed that the Church's relationship with the world would mean 'the setting free of the world into independence, intrinsic significance and autonomy'. And he went on to explain, 'Closeness to God and the world's own intrinsic reality are not inversely, but directly proportionate.'[20] In other words, he was saying, just as people become holy, not by becoming less human, but by becoming fully human, so the world achieves its God-given destiny, not by compromising its own proper identity, but by fulfilling it, by bringing it to completion. And that is the basis on which a healthy, mature relationship between the Church and the world can be built, one that will in its turn be able to generate a renewed sense of trust.

20 Karl Rahner, 'Church and World', in Adolf Darlap (ed.), *Sacramentum Mundi* i, (London, Burns and Oates, 1970), p.353.

Exercising power

Trust can also be restored by the way power is exercised, a way not based on control, but one that shows respect. The experience of a friend of mine will illustrate the point.

Some years ago he was appointed as head of a religious community. When he had been in post for some months, his provincial superior came to visit. He was pleased with what my friend had done and encouraged him, but he also offered a word of advice. 'They like you,' he told him, 'and are pleased with the way you have begun, but there are some complaints. They're not always sure what you expect of them. It makes them feel insecure, uncertain. They need greater clarity, more definite direction.' My friend recognised the wisdom in the advice. He realised, partly because of his own struggles in his new position, that there had been occasions when he could have made his intentions clearer. But, at the same time, he had no wish to supply exhaustive lists of precise instructions that might make people feel secure, but that would mean treating them like children. He took note of the provincial's advice, but followed it in moderation. Time passed. Some years later the provincial returned. He commented that the community was happy and thriving. He also reminded my friend of their earlier conversation. He recognised what had happened and was complimentary. 'They have caught your style,' he said. Building an atmosphere in which people feel valued creates a culture in which it seems natural to have confidence and be trusting. It is not achieved just by issuing commands, but by showing respect and inviting people to play their part.

★

To say it again, restoring trust that has been lost is never easy. It takes time. For the Church the situation has been desperate. A verse from the Book of Lamentations comes to mind: 'My soul is bereft of peace; I have forgotten what happiness is' (Lamentations 3:17). Yet if we go forward, seeking to make the Church as communion come to be truly alive, exploring our deepest desires, establishing healthy and mature relationships, and respecting and valuing people, then we may find other words from Lamentations becoming appropriate: 'This I call to mind, and therefore I have hope. The steadfast love of the Lord never ceases, his mercies never come to an end' (Lamentations 3:21–2).

14

Black stars shedding light

This journey into light ends in November. Elsewhere, of course, it is otherwise, but in the northern hemisphere that fact seems rather ironical. November is a grey month with lengthening nights, strong winds and heavy rain. It is also the time when we mourn those who have died, when we remember those who have fallen in war, and when we are invited to acknowledge our own destiny. We too will die and we will be judged. How are we to understand hell? How are we to understand heaven? Our mood may become as grey as the month. The prospect of judgment in particular may seem daunting, but we should not lose heart.

★

Consider judgment. As a young student in Rome in 1965, I was obliged to take a short course, studying some texts of Aristotle. The lectures were in Latin, as was customary in Rome at that time, and the oral exam at the end was also in Latin. When I was examined, the examiner indicated a passage that to my consternation I had not studied. I had believed it, no doubt mistakenly, not to have been one of the excerpts included on the syllabus. He asked me to read the first sentence which I did and then invited me to comment. My brain was numb. He suggested I read the second sentence which I then did, and discovered that it began to explain the first. In this way, sentence by sentence, I stumbled through my ten minutes of torture. When the results were published, I was astonished and relieved to find I had just scraped a pass.

Looking back, I smile at the experience, but I also wonder whether what happened to me on that occasion does not correspond to the way many people think of the judgment they will face when they die. Like me in that examination all those years ago, do they wonder whether they are going to be judged according to a syllabus, so to speak, of which they had been unaware? But that makes no sense. The syllabus cannot be a secret. The syllabus is well known to each of us. We are the syllabus. We have been born to be our true selves. One clue to self-knowledge might be to reflect on the three parables we find in the twenty-fifth chapter of Matthew's Gospel.

The first is the parable of the ten bridesmaids, five of whom, we are told, were foolish and five were wise. They were sent out with lamps to meet the bridegroom. The wise brought extra oil with them, so that their lamps would not go out, should the bridegroom be delayed. And he was. The foolish who hadn't bothered to bring extra oil then appealed to the wise to share their oil, but received a dusty answer: 'There may not be enough for us and for you.' Does that sound wise? Or were they just being mean? Why wouldn't they share what they had in reserve? Parables, however, are meant to teach specific lessons. This one is not about sharing; that will come later; this is a parable about the way we use resources. The foolish bridesmaids were negligent and wasteful. They had not brought extra oil and had squandered what they had. The wise used their oil with care. So the lesson we learn from this parable is to husband our resources, our talents, with care.

It makes no difference how rich we may be in talent. That is the lesson of the second parable: a man going on a journey divides his property so that it is cared for in his absence. To one servant he gives five talents, to another two, to a third just one. Some people have exceptional gifts; others appear poorly endowed; distribution is uneven. It is true that the servant who received the single talent is punished later, but not because he had that one talent alone, but because, like the foolish brides-maids, he had done nothing with it. However, what is more noteworthy is the fact that the servant with five talents has no advantage over the one with two. He had used those two wisely and is praised as warmly as the one who had been given five. No difference is made between them. That is the nub of the matter. Whatever our gifts, our talents, have we used them wisely?

And now we hear the third parable with which we are already familiar. It is the passage Pope Francis encouraged people to read at World Youth Day in 2013. And here indeed the lesson is about sharing. Our talents, our gifts, are not only for ourselves, but are to be used for the good of others as well. The familiar words toll out: have we fed the hungry, given drink to the thirsty, welcomed strangers, clothed the naked, and visited those who are sick or in prison? And in his encycli-cal letter, *Laudato Sì*, on care for our common home, Pope Francis reminds people how inseparable for his patron, St Francis of Assisi, is the bond between 'concern for nature, justice for the poor, commitment to society, and interior peace'.[1] The care we show is all connected.

As we recognise that one day we will die, we may wonder, especially during November, how wisely we have used our gifts, whether they be great or small, both on our own behalf and on behalf of others. Helping others, supplying food and drink, shelter and clothing, and visiting those in need, whether they are sick or in prison, indicates immediate, practical ways for us to be of use. And when we are generous, offering help and support, we encounter the Christ. Jesus said, 'Just as you did it to one of the least of these, you did it to me.' And we should bear in mind that we may encounter him not only in people, but also in situations. Just as in Advent we were

1 Pope Francis, *Laudato Sì*, n.10.

encouraged to be on the watch for his presence, so now, as the
year ends, we should still remain alert. We can do so as well on
Remembrance Day, when we recall those who have fallen in
war. Does that surprise us? Can Christ be present even amid
the horror and brutality of conflict? The question makes me
think of Jack McManners.

★

'War is about killing.' Those words, stating 'the elementary
reality', open McManners' account of the moment he found
himself seeing people for the first time who had been killed in
combat.[2] John McManners was to become a distinguished
Church historian and the Regius Professor of Ecclesiastical
History at Oxford University. This experience took place in
the desert to the south of Tobruk, while he was serving with
the Eighth Army in the Second World War.

He had been sent on his first reconnaissance with an Australian
captain to investigate a speck on the skyline and to find out
whether there was any sign of the enemy. He describes himself
as a complete novice and the captain as 'hardly battle-hardened'.
They set off cluelessly, he said, without map or binoculars, without cover and walking upright. When they realised that the
feature was in fact a sandbagged post, they started to crawl, and
when they looked over the parapet, 'there were about a dozen
dead Germans, slashed to bits with grenade fragments and bayo-
net thrusts'. That evening McManners wrote to John Brewis, his
former Oxford tutor, who was by then Principal of St Chad's
College in Durham, 'to say that, if I ever got back, I intended to
be ordained, and I wanted him to remind me'. In times of crisis,
we take stock: what matters to us?

What particularly appeals to me about this account is the
fact that after the war Brewis did indeed write, reminding Jack

2 John McManners, *Fusilier: Recollections and Reflections, 1939–1945*,
(London, Michael Russell, 2002), p.59.

of his intention and offering him a place at St Chad's. McManners acknowledges, however, that his resolution by then had collapsed and his heart was no longer convinced: 'The decision had been taken at the first sight of sudden, savage death, of the cruelty of man to man,' he observed. 'I had seen many more dead men now.' But Brewis persuaded him at least to study theology for two years.

Gradually the intellectual fascination with theology, accompanied by some praying, became something else, not cloying piety, but an awareness of human evil, displayed in that sandbagged post at Tobruk. McManners commented that behind the business world that others identify as real is the *real* world they have forgotten, 'the battlefield'. And so he found himself turning to Jesus on the cross, 'to the God who suffers with his creation, accepting the burden of sin that arises from human freedom, and taking it on himself'. In spite of this conviction, ordination was not automatic. But then came an invitation to pastoral and academic duties, as chaplain and tutor at his old Oxford college. 'So I was ordained,' he concluded with self-deprecating humour, 'like the port-filled dons of old, to go to a Fellowship.'[3]

There are various ways of interpreting Jack McManners' reaction to savage violence in the desert. But perhaps that reaction and its aftermath, disguised by humour, were graces, prompted by a watchfulness of which even he was scarcely aware.

★

On the watch in November we think indeed about death, but also about life after death. Ludovic Kennedy died in 2009. An intelligent, impressive, cultured man, with a burning passion for justice, he was also a committed atheist. In one of his obituaries I was struck to read that one reason in particular for his

3 McManners, *Fusilier*, pp.213, 217–18.

atheism was the death of his father at sea during the Second World War. It was said to illustrate for him 'the uselessness of prayer'. His father, he once explained, 'had a very simple faith. He prayed every night and morning of his life, and I know he would have done that in the morning of the battle, and look what happened to him.' The loss of those we love can be excruciating and bewildering. When people grieve, we try to comfort them, not pass judgment. There is no question of that here. Yet I wonder that so intelligent a man as Kennedy should regard prayer as valid only when it operates as a kind of guarantee against disaster, so that, when tragedy occurs in spite of our praying, the value of prayer is nullified and the path into a life without faith in God and so without hope in life after death is somehow validated.

Another reason for abandoning faith when one considers life after death is the notion of eternity as quite literally life that lasts for ever. The philosopher Anthony Kenny has described as troubling the possibility of life continuing after death. 'It is not just that annihilation would be vastly preferable to the torments of the damned,' he has observed; 'it is that even painless perpetuity would be appalling.'[4] Tony Kenny is not a theist, but neither does he regard himself as an atheist. Life everlasting, however, can also alarm those who have faith. The writer Teresa McLean has said, 'I believe in God, but the thought of eternity fills me with horror: I dread the thought of anything, even heaven, going on without end.'[5]

The difficulty revolves around duration. People recoil from the tedium of life simply going on and on. Life without end seems deeply unattractive. But perhaps the difficulty arises not least because all our experience takes place within time and

4 Anthony Kenny, *What I Believe*, (London, Continuum, 2006), p.165.
5 Teresa McLean, *Metal Jam: The Story of a Diabetic*, (London, Hodder and Stoughton, 1985), p.145.

our way of speaking automatically reflects that. We strain to imagine anything different. Thus eternal life, life after death, becomes life everlasting. But it helps to remember, however difficult it may be to imagine, that the next chapter of our existence is not shackled to duration. Beyond this life we move beyond time and perhaps with care we may glimpse even within our time-bound experience traces of what life beyond time might be like. Let me offer two examples, one of hell, the other of heaven.

Teresa McLean's horror of eternity may have been prompted by her experience of diabetes. In 1985 she told the story in her compelling book, *Metal Jam*. There she describes waking one morning in winter paralysed. Then her ordeal began.

She needed sugar from the kitchen. She managed somehow to fall out of bed and crawl to the stairs. Hoping to slide down, in fact she tumbled, bruising ribs, cracking her head, and blacking out. When she came to, everything hurt. She dragged herself across the floor to the kitchen, but realised she could not reach the sugar bowl on the ledge. Instead she tugged at the lead on the coffee percolator, because there was sugar near it, dragging it down over her and the sugar with it. She lay on the floor amid a flood of coffee which turned the sugar brown. In desperation she licked it from the floor, but then vomited. Feeling worse than ever, she rallied and managed to nudge the sugar bowl to the kitchen door, which somehow she opened. Then, lifting the sugar bowl over the doorstep with her teeth, she crawled into the garden, dropping the bowl into the snow that was lying on the ground and swallowing mouthfuls of snow, now full of sugar. She was surprised not to be sick again and gradually began to recover.

This account abbreviates and therefore inevitably sanitises her nightmarish experience. When I read what she wrote for the first time, I remember wondering how someone could survive such an ordeal. It seemed to last for hours. In fact, as she recovered, she realised it had lasted no more than ten minutes.[6]

A happier story can be told more briefly. Visiting once a man whose wife had just died, I heard about the time he had discovered that he loved her. They had known each other for years as part of a group of friends. One evening, after dinner out, the others had drifted off and they were left alone. Without warning the conversation suddenly plunged to another level and they became completely absorbed in each other, talking on and on. By the end they recognised a bond of love between them that was indestructible. And so it had proved. 'But then,' he added, 'I glanced at my watch and realised we'd been talking for less than an hour.'

In both cases the intensity of the experience, one of misery, the other of joy, had made a little time seem long. Now take that further, to the ultimate point.

In eternity, beyond time, we slip the chains of duration. Our relationships are realised perfectly. Heaven is the perfection of loving. We are free, of course, to choose to resist love and reject God's mercy so as to be caught in that moment of isolated misery we call hell. But those who choose otherwise are in paradise. Nor, I would suggest, does their love for God obliterate their love for those whom they have loved and lost. Dread of perpetual separation can make that loss all the more agonising. It is a dread people often express. But loving is not a competition. To be overwhelmed by love for God is not to lose interest in loving anyone else. On the contrary, loving God, we are able to embrace in love in the eternal, heavenly instant all those whom we hold dear.

*

A firm faith in life after death, however, does not soften the sense of loss when someone dear to us dies. That makes me think of Alfredo Piacentini who died in January 2004.

6 See McLean, *Metal Jam*, pp. 198–202.

Alfredo was born in 1922 at Palazzola, the summer villa in the Alban Hills outside Rome which is owned by the English College where people are prepared for ordination to priest-hood. His father had become its caretaker in 1920 and Alfredo helped and succeeded him. Throughout his long life, in peace and in war, Alfredo cared for Palazzola, utterly faithful, utterly loyal to the College, its staff and students. Those of us who knew him, owe him more than we probably realise. Many stories are told about Alfredo's life, but there is also a story about his dying that deserves to be remembered.

As he lay apparently unconscious and close to death with his family gathered round him, his grandson, Riccardo, who was nineteen years of age and particularly close to his grandfather, took his hand and Alfredo gripped his thumb. After a long time, however, Riccardo had to leave. His thumb was prised gently from Alfredo's grasp, and a tear rolled down the old man's cheek.

Soon after, Alfredo died. Riccardo, deeply distressed, was comforted by his mother. Finally she said to him, 'You saw how ill your grandfather was. You wouldn't have wanted him to continue in that condition.' The young man thought for a moment and then nodded his head. 'Yes, I would,' he said. When those whom we love die, the physical separation can seem unbearable. Their absence fuels our grief. These deaths can leave scars and sometimes they throb. Iris Murdoch once observed, 'There are times of suffering which remain in our lives like black absolutes, and are not blotted out.' But then she continued, 'Fortunate are those for whom these black stars shed some sort of light',[7] words that evidently have prompted the title for this chapter.

That light may be found by praying for those who have died. These prayers are not a mere sop for our sorrow. In

7 These words appear as an epigraph to a volume of Paul Murray's poems, *These Black Stars,* (The Dedalus Press, 2003).

Eamon Duffy's memorable explanation, 'The Church's faith is that in Christ the loneliness of death is overcome. Whatever the circumstances of our dying, the reality is that none of us dies alone, we are surrounded and supported by the prayers of the Church, a support which continues into the silence of death.'[8] The pain of separation may not be wiped away; there are no magical formulas for banishing grief; but prayer maintains and strengthens the bonds between us and can inspire us with hope. And so the black stars shed their light. Let me offer one final, as it seems to me, luminous example.

*

In the 1980s on Boars' Hill outside Oxford, someone gave me a document that is serene and full of hope. I have treasured it ever since. For many years I could not remember who gave it to me, but drafting this chapter I wanted to reproduce it because it seemed to me that it is not simply a private statement, but rather a statement that is intended without pretension to bear witness powerfully to deep faith. It is signed, 'L. Roper-Power', and called 'Lilian's Testament', so, I assumed, the person who composed it was indeed Lilian Roper-Power. It is dated 15 July 1972. Then an idea occurred to me and I thought of a friend, Catherine Bernard, who had lived on Boars' Hill and might remember who Lilian was. The name struck a chord with her and she asked members of her family for help. Very soon she had contacted Lilian's surviving children who kindly agreed to let me reproduce it here. I do so with gratitude because this testament distils so much of the disposition to which these November reflections have been leading.

8 Eamon Duffy, *Faith of our Fathers: Reflections on Catholic Tradition*, (London, Continuum, 2004), p.131.

LILIAN'S TESTAMENT

This month of July 1972 – being full well in my mind, but convalescing, and weary in body – and having had long hours in which to think quietly, remember, give thanks for much happiness – (this is the eve of the 34th anniversary of our wedding . . .) and meditate on the future – I should like to put down some of these thoughts . . . And I pray that the present peace of mind and heart and joy with which I write these words on this perfect summer day may still shine through them when they are read.

I cannot know when, where, nor how death will come to me; but may I be granted the grace to meet it with simplicity and dignity – however hard and humbling and lonely the struggle of the body may be. I believe that my spirit will live, that the moment of death will be the moment of truth, and that in a flash we shall know the order and purpose of the divine plan and enter into fulfilment and perfect union with God.

It is no good trying to 'explain' . . . Faith is illogical. All I know is that I believe. For me, and the more so as I grow older, the Christian religion has 'made sense' of things; the Incarnation and the Cross defeat evil and despair. I am deeply conscious of belonging to a great Communion of Saints – of all ages and places – and I am grateful to have been born into the great Christian tradition; I have always loved its order, its wisdom, its compassion, and I have loved the Church for the sanity of its teachings, and the beauty of its monuments and rites.
In manus tuas, Domine, commendo spiritum meum.

I want my body to return to the earth, and the grass to grow over the simplest of wooden crosses. I want no bought flowers, no mourning, no tokens of remembrance. But I would very much desire a Requiem Mass to be said, to bring repose to my soul, and I hope peace and serenity to those who will hear it. 'And all shall be well, and all manner of thing shall be well.'

15

Into light

November is not exclusively grey. Its black stars shed startling light as the month begins and again towards its end. On the first day of the month we celebrate the feast of All Saints and on a Sunday towards the month's end we celebrate the feast of Christ the King. Those occasions lift these final days of the liturgical year and shine through the gloom. As we come to the end of this journey into light, both feasts engage our attention.

*

All Saints

In Italy the feast of All Saints is a national holiday. Even if the United Kingdom is not as secular as people sometimes suppose, the idea of a day set aside to honour saints may seem bizarre. But when we call people saints, what are we saying? Our ideas are often confused.

One cause for this confusion may be found in our understanding of what holiness entails. All unawares, we may be snared in a contradiction. In the popular imagination a saint is often regarded as someone who is perfect. There have indeed been lives written about saints that stoke up such a view, uncritical hagiography that is unrealistic and ridiculous. It brings the very idea of sanctity into disrepute. And so it becomes easy to dismiss the notion of personal holiness altogether, for whenever failings are found, which they always are, it follows that that individual cannot be a saint. Scepticism stands proud. Of course, the irony is that, according to that criterion, someone could only be accepted as holy who reflected the very hagiography that is recognised as absurd. But holiness is not a matter of idealised perfection. Saints make mistakes and commit sins. It helps to remember an observation of Pope Benedict's at one of his public audiences in 2007, when he remarked that 'the saints have not "fallen from Heaven". They are people like us, who also have complicated problems. Holiness does not consist in never having erred or sinned.'[1] Saints, however, are not complacent. They struggle to overcome their weaknesses, defects and sins. That is why they are models for us. And as they struggle also to be themselves, to be committed in love, they bring their humanity, whole and entire, into communion with the Spirit of Christ.

Such language, 'communion with the Spirit of Christ', may be another cause of confusion. It makes holiness seem rarefied, unusual, outside our experience. But is it? Many years ago, I was invited to give a talk about saints. I spoke partly about the origin of devotion to the saints, to those early saints who usually were martyrs, men and women who had died rather than deny their faith, and then I reflected on devotion to those who came later who were honoured after persecutions had largely come to an end. Some of these were teachers, for example, others were hermits. Then afterwards, during the time for discussion, a woman stood up and thanked me, but she also pointed out that there was one group I had omitted. 'You haven't mentioned the saints we know,' she said. 'I think my grandmother was a saint.' She was not just being pious or sentimental about a member of her family. She was making a valuable point and I have never forgotten it. Holiness does not

1 See *L'Osservatore Romano*, Weekly Edition in English, 7 February 2007, p.11.

need to be as rare as we sometimes suppose. There are many people who are saints, even though they may never be recognised as such formally by the Church. Saints are models of Christian living.

Readers of these pages may realise that mine would include Donald Nicholl and Mary David Totah. As to Mary David, those wondering about my reasons should read her writings, especially *The Joy of God*, and they will also find at the end of the book the account by the infirmarian at St Cecilia's Abbey, Sister Elizabeth Burgess, of Mary David's last days and her dying, accepted with joy. Mary David had once remarked, perhaps unwisely, to her abbess, 'I hope God will ask a lot of me.' And God, it seems, had taken her at her word. And, as to Donald, his presence for me at least cast light on what it must have been like to be in the company of Jesus. There must have been something compelling about it. As it was impossible to lie to Donald, or behave hypocritically, or pretend to have a knowledge you did not have, because the hollowness and artificiality, the unreality, would have been evident to him at once – so it would have been impossible in the presence of Jesus. I felt Donald's presence had that Christ-like quality.

Who are your Donalds and Mary Davids?

Saints make no claims for themselves. They know that they have been weak and have sinned. They see themselves as doing no more than their duty. They do it gladly, willingly, faithfully, and unselfconsciously, whatever the cost. To put the matter another way, as Jesus remarked, it is those who exalt themselves who will be humbled and those who humble themselves who will be exalted (Matthew 23:12). There have been more saints in our midst than we have realised, ordinary people, otherwise unacknowledged. They have been the heartbeat of a healthy society. And they are the people who now have died and for whom we give thanks on the feast of All Saints.

★

Christ the King

Monarchy suggests magnificence, grandeur, and privilege, but the feast of Christ the King is shorn of those qualities. The rumour of kingship, however, runs like wildfire through the stubble in the Gospel narrative.

According to Matthew, it was news of a king's birth that caused Herod to order the massacre of the innocents. When Jesus began his ministry, he did so by proclaiming that the kingdom of heaven was close at hand, while many of his parables, and one series in particular that we considered earlier, explored that proclamation. In due course, he was welcomed into Jerusalem as a king and the charge was levelled against him during his trial some days later. On his cross were nailed the words, 'Jesus of Nazareth, the King of the Jews'. That notice may have been prompted by cynicism, but the question remains, what kind of king was he? He was the kind revealed by the kingdom he sought to establish and he is made known to us in the three Gospel passages particularly associated with this feast.

In the first, when interrogated by Pilate and asked whether he was a king, Jesus replied, 'My kingdom is not from this world. If my kingdom were from this world, my followers would be fighting to keep me from being handed over to the Jews. But as it is, my kingdom is not from here.' Pilate then pressed him further, asking, 'So you are a king?' And Jesus replied, 'You say that I am a king. For this I was born, and for this I came into the world, to testify to the truth. Everyone who belongs to the truth listens to my voice.' And it was then that Pilate commented, perhaps cynically or perhaps just wearily, 'What is truth?' (John 18:33–8).

This truth is not something abstract. Besides Pilate's interrogation, a second passage offered for reflection on this feast is one that has recurred several times in these pages, the account of the Son of Man coming as king and as judge. The questions by now should be familiar: have we fed the hungry, given drink to the thirsty, welcomed the stranger, clothed the naked, and visited those who are sick or in prison? Has our care for others been practical? For the king, as we know, identifies himself with those who are in need: 'Truly I tell you, just as you did it to one of the least of these who are members of my family, you did it to me' (Matthew 25:40).

Then in the third passage the king is seen, not at all as magnificent, grand and privileged, but himself nailed to a cross between two thieves. One of them abused him. 'Are you not the Messiah?' he sneered. 'Save yourself and us.' But the other rebuked him and asked Jesus, 'Remember me when you come into your kingdom.' And Jesus replied, 'Today you will be with me in Paradise' (Luke 23:39–43).

These three passages from three different Gospels nevertheless reveal a coherent vision of Christ as King: he is a king, but not of this world; he identifies himself with those who are most in need; and when he is in need himself, dying on the cross, he is still offering mercy to the man dying beside him.

★

In the legend of the Holy Grail, there is a Fisher King who is wounded because he has sinned and his kingdom is laid waste. In the Gospels, Jesus is the Shepherd King who is wounded, not because he has sinned, but because we have. He has taken on himself our wounded condition so that the wasteland may be restored and the desert bloom. His kingdom is not a territory, but a people. The preface that is prayed before the Eucharistic Prayer at Mass on this day describes this kingdom as a kingdom of truth and life, of holiness and grace, of justice, love and peace. These are powerful words, humbling words. Who would dare to claim citizenship in such a kingdom? Our failings are so evident. But these words can also remind us of the nature and dignity of our calling.

Consider, first, holiness and grace. These words, we know, can be understood as code words for the inner life of God. To be holy and full of grace is to share in God's life. The notion may seem absurd or extravagant. It may certainly take our breath away. But then we should remember those words spoken by Jesus in the Sermon on the Mount: 'Be perfect, therefore, as your heavenly Father is perfect' (Matthew 5:48). I have often wondered how much anxiety, how much scrupulosity, those words have caused, especially among people of a certain temperament who have striven for the ideal of divine perfection and found themselves constantly falling short. What they have failed to notice is that crucial word, 'therefore'.

This saying is not so much a command as a conclusion. It is particular and practical. Jesus has been instructing the crowds not to confine their generosity to their families and friends, nor to limit their contacts to those who will serve their self-interest; instead they are to love their enemies and pray for those who seek to harm them. They are to treat people equally. That is the Father's way, 'for he makes his sun rise on the evil and on the good, and sends rain on the righteous and the unrighteous' (Matthew 5:45). That is the disposition that reflects the inner life of God, the kind of perfection to which we are called. It is evidence of holiness and grace.

It leads to a society built on love. This love, we have realised, is more than mere emotion, more than a matter of cultivating further an affinity with kindred spirits. It derives, as we have noticed elsewhere already, from decision, that is from the deep desire to live in a way that seeks out even those who are not congenial to us or may in fact be hostile so as to overcome conflict and be reconciled. It values justice and works for peace. Lives rooted in holiness and grace bear fruit in love and justice and peace. Moreover, they cannot be faked. Lives lived in this way ring true.

Many years ago, when 'integrity' had become something of a vogue word, a philosopher friend wondered one day, tongue-in-cheek, what it meant. However casually indiscriminate its use may have been at that time, it may be understood not least as referring to a combination of different qualities so as to make a coherent whole, such as a kingdom of holiness and grace, of justice, love and peace, and of truth and life. That is the kingdom of Jesus Christ, our Shepherd King. It is our destination as we journey into light.

Index

References to images are in *italics*.